Sheet Music
to My Accoustic
Nightmare

Stephanie M. Wytovich

RAW DOG SCREAMING PRESS

Sheet Music to My Accoustic Nightmare ©2017 by Stephanie M. Wytovich

Previously published::

Pittsburgh City Paper. "Accidental Love Note." Chapter&Verse. Web. 2016.

Three Drops Poetry. Samhain Special. "At an Apothecary in New Orleans." Web. 2016.

Poetry Breakfast. ""Before Leaving Ireland, Summer of 2015" and "Breaking Glass on the Way to Accidentally Falling in Love." Web. 2016.

Robert Morris University. "The Fireworks Were Wet in 2011." *Rune Literary Magazine.* Print. 2016.

Spectral Realms Magazine. "Head Ornaments" and "Girls and Their Balloons." Print. 2015.

Sanitarium Magazine. "Of My Wounds, There are Many." Issue 48. Web. 2016.

Burial Day Books. "The Moon Makes Love to Shadows," "Two of Swords," and "Winter Canvas." Print. 2015.

Published by Raw Dog Screaming Press
Bowie, MD

All rights reserved.

First Edition

Cover illustration: Steven Archer
Book design: M. Garrow Bourke

ISBN: 978-1-947879-003
Library of Congress Control Number: 2017961591

Printed in the United States of America

www.RawDogScreaming.com

Contents

Author's Note 10
3:48 a.m. Trespassing in My Lover's Bed 14
395 Miles to Lost Memories 15
Accidental Love Note 16
Add Him to the Playlist of the Times I Died 17
After We Sleep It Off 18
All the Angels in My Life Are Broken 19
At an Apothecary in New Orleans 20
Because I'm Stained Red 21
Becoming a Pyromaniac After Learning What the Word Meant 22
Before Leaving Ireland, Summer of 2015 23
Beneath the Animals of Dark 24
Beware the Witch Bottle in My Kitchen 25
Breaking Glass on the Way to Accidentally Falling in Love 26
Burial Instructions to Hide the Body 27
Camera on the Dashboard, Body in the Trunk 28
Cancel the Reservations 29
Catcalling at the Devil in Sin City 30
Chase the Morning with a Spoonful of Failure 31
Crossroads Are for Lovers Who Aren't Yet Enemies 32
David Bowie is Dead 33
Default Black 34
Departure 35
Desperate Choices 36
Driving the Road to Nowhere Fast 38
Energy Songs in a Texas Swamp 39
Emergency Masturbation Fantasy 40
Escaping the Forest, I Found My Voice 41
Exit Wounds in His Kiss, Your Memory 42
Extracting Ectoplasm from Freshly Dug Corpses 43
Filleting My Body for Old Time's Sake 44
Forcing My Ghost on Monastery Grounds 45
Forgetting How to Form New Memories 46

Full Dark, Only Black	47
Funeral in August of 2016	48
Give Me a Reason to Sing	49
Go Set the Ghosts to Possession	50
Grabbing for Cigarettes, Grabbing for Teeth	51
Gravity Glue for Chakra Health	52
Guitar Players Wear Pain Like I Wear Stilettos	53
Hanging Imaginary Drapes in Jefferson Hospital	54
Head Ornaments	55
Hitchhiking to Stop the Voices	56
How the 80s Taught Me About Trauma Bonding	57
Hunted Down from the Other Side	58
I Am Not Your Daughter	60
I Build Versions of You That Won't Leave	61
In a Name, There are Ten Thousand Lies	62
Iron and Silver Accent Her Life	63
It's Raining in February and I Can't Find God	64
Jail Time for Harboring a Fugitive	65
Janis Joplin is My Spirit Animal Half-Past Dead	66
Joyriding into the City We Burned Down	67
Just Let Me Go to Gone	68
Just like the First Time I Caught Fire	69
Karma Tells Me What She Did to You	70
Keg Stands and Car Accidents at Gunpoint	71
Key Places to Lose Your Blood	72
Killing Floor	73
Kneecaps for Lunch	74
Lanterns Hang at Feeding Time	75
Leftover Slaughter for Two	76
Life, Interrupted	77
Like Smoke, Like Fog	78
Looking for the Headless Driver	79
Making Snow Angels Out of Songs of Madness	80
Married to the Idea of My Death	81

Memory Retrieval, 1991, Finleyville, PA 82
My Apologies, I'm Dead 84
My Underwear Choice Wasn't for Him 85
Naked in a Motel Room with Spilled Wine 86
Navigating Family History 87
Near the Stairwell in the Dungeon 88
Nocturnal Bee Song 89
Numb in April 90
Of My Wounds, There Are Many 91
On Listening to "Dressed in Smoke" at 11:12 p.m. 93
On Listening to Nick Cave's "Jubilee Street" 95
On the Other Side of the Glass 96
Outside While I Waited 97
Past-Life Regression Therapy, c. 1800 98
Pirate Gospel 99
Post-Traumatic Spiders 100
Pressing Charges 101
Pretty Little Things 102
Quality Control 103
Quarterly Letters Never Sent 104
Quay's Brought Bon Jovi to Dublin 105
Quit the Night, Lick the Morning 106
Quoting My Dead Angels 107
Raven's Rock 108
Reasons I Don't Ride Motorcycles Anymore 109
Removing Past Lives 110
Requiem for Love Lost and Love Gained 111
Rest Stop off of the Psycho Path 113
Runaway Bride 115
Second Place to a Musician's First Love 117
Seduced by Monsters 118
Self-Study in Pornography 119
Sheet Music to My Acoustic Nightmare 121
She Filled a Music Box Full of Bad Dreams 123

The Fireworks Were Wet in 2011	124
The First Time I Thought of Suicide, I was on the Toilet	125
There's a Gypsy in My Chest	126
The Moon Makes Love to Shadows	127
Two of Swords	128
Ugly Little Things, Aren't They?	130
Under Take Her	131
Under the Dirt Blanket	132
Unwelcomed Decisions on the 5:30 p.m. Blue Line	134
Unwinding the Black Outs	135
Validated PTSD, Therapy Session #4	137
Valkyrie Training for the Day	139
Verifying Bodies After Car Crashes	140
Versions of My Mutilated Self	141
Violins Bring the Serpents	143
Wearing Red Lipstick and Skyping with the Wolf	144
What I Brought with Me on the Plane	145
What it Takes to Sing the Blues	146
When I Promised Him Murder	147
Winter Canvas	149
Yawning While Driving Down 61'	151
Yearly Bath for a Tired Heart	152
Yelling in My Sleep	153
Young Wolves Take to the Night	154
Your Ghost	155
Zero Regrets Party Crashing	156
Zest for the Afterbite	157
Zigzagging Through Asylum Snowflakes	158
Ziploc Bag Full of Dead Butterflies	159
Zombie-Syndrome in a Foreign City	160
About the Author	161

Dedication

For my family.
With love.

Mom, Dad, and Scott
We have survived an immeasurable amount of pain together.
Thank you for never giving up on me, even when you should have.

Acknowledgements

WITHOUT THE HELP, SUPPORT, AND love of my friends and family, I wouldn't have had the courage, strength, or persistence to write this book, which is half memoir, half fiction.

To Jennifer Barnes, my fellow daughter of darkness, for being a wonderful friend and colleague. Thank you for listening to me process, ramble, vent, cry, and brainstorm. I quite literally couldn't have done, or gotten though, any of this without you. You're my rock.

To John Edward Lawson for giving me movie homework and sending me clown pictures every morning to make me laugh. I appreciate your ability to always make me smile.

To Michelle Renee Lane for the phone calls, the movie nights, the drinks and late night discussions. I thank the universe every day that I know you.

To Matthew O'Dwyer for encouraging me to be the best version of myself and for writing me handwritten letters to show me that distance doesn't matter when you find true friendship.

To Ryan DeMoss for jumping on a plane and meeting me in Los Angeles without a moment's hesitation. Your kindness and ability to pull me out of the darkness is one of the many things I love about you. You're such a bright, happy spot in my life.

To Austin Black for keeping me sane, for wiping my tears, for telling me that I'm beautiful, and for holding my hand through one of the hardest times of my life. There are no words to tell you how much I love you for what you've done for me.

To Kristin Dearborn for traveling the country with me, sharing stories and lousy rooms in Las Vegas, and for feeding me gummy sludge and taking me to Massachusetts for coffee when I needed it the most. The next round of pineapples is on me.

To Scott, my brother, for listening when I couldn't talk, for holding me when I couldn't stand, for always telling me that it would be okay, even when we both knew it wouldn't. I might be the older sibling, but you've always protected me and kept me safe, told me when to hide and yelled for me when it was time to run. I knew from the moment I first held you when you were born that we would be best friends, and I'm glad to know that I was right.

I owe you all a lifetime of love and thanks.
—*Stephanie M. Wytovich*

Author's Note

I FIRST GOT THE IDEA for this version of *Sheet Music to My Acoustic Nightmare* a couple years ago while I was sleeping in an unfinished house with nothing next to me but empty beer bottles, some cigarettes and Sheetz containers, and my then-ex-boyfriend who just so happened to be stealing all of the one blanket we had on us. The sun was barely up. I was awake breathing sawdust and craving coffee, and all I could think about in that moment was how I was having the time of my life while simultaneously dying in a hell I never knew I had the power to create.

As I write this note in August of 2016, my muse has been locked in that house for a little over two years, and I hear her screaming and crying in there almost every morning when I wake up. You see, Jolene and I met long before that night. She's been there every time I got in my car to drive away, and every instance since where I've invited in a similar, lingering type of misdirection. I had become a pro at running, and to this day, I always know when it's time to leave because life has taught me all about escaping, about hiding and forgetting. From a young age, I had to camouflage my instincts from demons both real and imaginary, and as I grew up, I had to disguise my heart into something that even when broken, still had the appearance of something that worked. Jolene sang with me as I cried during those road trips and she held my hand while I hallucinated on those highways. Sometimes when I slept at a rest stop, she'd stand watch outside the car to make sure no one broke in, and on rare occasions, she'd slip into my nightmares and try to ease the pain.

> *But when the day turned off and the stars went out, Jolene took care of business with death-bed confessions and midnight beggings. She cut off sentences and drained blood nto buckets, buckets she used to drown wanted men and unhinged monsters...*

You see, a good part of who I am as a writer is because of those times I spent on the road, the nights I spent telling stories to myself to stay awake, the early mornings I spent praying to red lights to change faster so I could get back to some version of what I called home. Jolene put blankets around my arms when my car broke down in Columbus, and she held my hand during rainstorms in Pittsburgh when I stalled out on bridges, but most importantly, she's kissed me goodnight and wrote lyrics to my fears, hoping that at some point when I was ready, I could try to heal.

> But when the dead ends appeared and the stop signs caught fire, Jolene dug graves and hid guitar cases, smothered songs and snuffed out fires because if I knew how she was protecting me, if I for one second suspected that maybe she wasn't my angel, but something darker, something cursed...

This collection is me trying to put back the pieces that have broken over my lifetime. I wanted to write a book about the years that I've spent on the road getting myself into trouble with ghosts and with men, all the while still writing about the nights where I got lost in bars and stranded in the middle of nowhere surrounded by nothing but bones and magic, blood and guitar strings. Yes, between these pages are stories about heartbreak and visions, about music and cowboys. It's my homage to westerns and my suicide note to horror, and it shows you my spirits, my hallucinations, shares with you my sheet music and my nightmares. These poems are my favorite haunts that I would tell in exchange for free drinks and stolen kisses, and they've been my ticket to redemption, my one shot at easing old regrets. They are pieces of prayers that I've written at crossroads, just as much as they are dares from attractive strangers and blood ballads to all the memories that have threatened to kill me at one point or another. They are my apologies to myself and to my incubus, to my lovers and my dead, because regardless if God was ever there with me or not, the one person who has always sung louder and always wrote a better version of the blues, is the woman who sits next to me telling me to run, to keep running, to never look back....

> Because to some degree I know, know that there are bodies in my trunk, and dirt on my shoes, and if I whisper in your ear that everything is going to be okay, I can promise you that's the sweetest lie I've ever told, because

Jolene can't be trusted, not when my soul is on the line, so you my friends, you should run. Run far and run fast. Because she doesn't like to watch me bleed, doesn't like to see me in pain, and when the lights go out and the music starts playing…

It's already too late.

—Stephanie M. Wytovich

"The need to go astray, to be destroyed, is an extremely private, distant, passionate, turbulent truth."
—Georges Bataille

"She had acquired some of his gypsy ways, some of his nonchalance, his bohemian indiscipline. She had swung with him into the disorders of strewn clothes, spilled cigarette ashes, slipping into bed all dressed, falling asleep thus, indolence, timelessness...A region of chaos and moonlight. She liked it there."
— Anaïs Nin

"It all ends in tears anyway."
—Jack Kerouac

3:48 a.m. Trespassing in My Lover's Bed

When we slept next to each other, 3:48 a.m.
blankets built like walls, pillows stacked as defense mechanisms,
I thought back to the nights I slept on the hardwood floors,
my jean jacket as my pillow while I cried off the high I self-induced
hours before. I remember being afraid then. Wondering if someone would
come into the house, arrest me for trespassing. For days, I peed in the woods,
woke up in the morning, drove into town, and in a McDonald's on East
   Pittsburgh Street,
I'd give myself a whore bath, take a dump, and order a coffee that was big
enough for two people.

Now I think how silly that sounds,
how laying here in complete safety is so much worse. If I run away,
the feelings are still there. If I want coffee, I can make it in the kitchen.
When I asked my ex-boyfriend why we broke into abandoned houses,
he said it was because they were all he had to offer. When I asked my current lover
why he slept in the next room, he said he was more comfortable being away
   from me.

And I remember waking up and screaming on my lover's couch. I ate cold pizza
   and told myself
stories that made me cry. I thought about my wedding day, a day I knew wouldn't
happen, just like how I knew I wouldn't have children. I looked out his window
   and fantasized
about leaving, about how someday if I had the courage to walk, maybe I
   wouldn't hurt;
that's how I dealt with my pain; I'd force myself to walk away, even if I'd never
   forget his face.

395 Miles to Lost Memories

The steering wheel holds a toothless grin.
Black gums beneath rotting lips,
It laughs louder with each mile I drive;

The windows hold the fog of the night.
Shattered glass beneath broken knuckles,
It burrows deeper with each missed call.

>And I can't see you in my rearview mirror anymore,
>Can't hear you singing in the backseat;
>*Did I leave you at the gas station in Cincinnati?*
>*Did I forget to pick you up in Pittsburgh?*

My radio is playing our song on repeat.
Guitar riffs and static between memorized lyrics,
It digs out the pain as I cross state borders;

My tires are bald from the stress of the road.
Two circles screaming from repetitious cycles,
They beg me to drive in the opposite direction.

>But I can't feel you with me as I stop for coffee,
>Can't taste the morning breath on your kiss;
>*Did I leave you in the trash I threw away at the truck stop?*
>*Did I forget to remember your ghost?*

Accidental Love Note

Paperclips and highway ghostings,
There's no sense of place just like there's no hint of sound;
The rotors fail and the car stalls, your phone number in ink
On the inside of my palm.

Gas station coffee, two empty cans,
There's this outside feeling, just like there's this devil may care;
My door is open, there's no one to call, your phone number in ink
On the inside of my palm.

Cigarette butts and shattered bottles,
There's a trail to the guardrail, just like there's a trail to the bridge;
The water whispers, the jump looks calm, your phone number in ink
On the inside of my palm.

Add Him to the Playlist of the Times I Died

95 miles per hour with clipped breaks and a death wish
down 64 West, I screamed the lyrics to songs I didn't know
while the Devil braided my hair in the passenger seat. I'd
gotten lost on purpose while sipping that Old No. 7 Brand,
left my jacket at a gas pump where I took off my shirt to
get away from the heat. I had no reason to be here, nowhere to go
but away, but Lucifer promised that my hair would attract flowers,
that I'd collect memories at the bottom of the river, and when I saw
the bridge, I turned up the music. I didn't have to wonder
who'd save my soul that night.

After We Sleep It Off

After we sleep it off,
maybe we can learn how to love each other again and
remember the night we went to the basement of your old house,
threw beer bottles against the cinder block walls and laid down in the glass
letting it cut into our backs so we could be each other's scars.

There's a chance that when we sober up,
that we'll forget everything the other said,
that my eyes won't be bloodshot, and your hands
will have stopped shaking long enough for us to see the good
that's masked beneath the damage others left behind.

Maybe when we wake up,
you'll be able to touch me without crying and
I'll be able to give myself to you without feeling abused,
perhaps I'll tell you I love you in the fantasy languages we both memorized,
make you breakfast while you grind the coffee beans I accidentally bought
at the store while I was high.

After we sleep it off,
maybe we can start us all over again and
remember the night I sat crying in your lap telling you
how much you meant to me and how scared I was of losing you,
and you telling me you weren't worth it, but that deep down
you couldn't help falling in love with me, too.

All the Angels in My Life Are Broken

Broken like the porcelain angels I knocked over
when I was six, I sat in my car thinking about how
I got here, about how I rolled up my sleeves
and drove for hours on a highway trying to find something
to put my pieces back together again.

Rewind to 1995:

I was playing ball in the house after Mom told me not to,
but I'm a careful advocate for the devil, and I thought
I was safe; it's almost funny now—my life story played out
in childhood memories. They fell from the shelves one by one
exploding against the hardwood floor like celestial bombs,
their faces shattered, erased,
my face frozen, silent.

Fast-forward to 2016:

My hands grip the steering wheel and my expression
is still the scared child who murdered
a flight of angels all those years ago. I throw my cross
out the window, light the cigarette that's been keeping
behind my ear. When I pray, it's in my poetry, and I
can almost hear the dead angels laugh.

At an Apothecary in New Orleans

She wore a silver dollar around her neck,
had the bones of a muskrat in her purse
when she laughed people looked our way
she'd spit in their direction and wink
   Are you sure this is what you want?
   Promise you won't hate yourself come morning?

I wore a whiskey grin and seven silver rings,
had the dreams of a junkie in my back pocket
when I spoke it sounded like wet ash slapping gravel
I'd cough and often cry from the right side of my face
   Give me the magic, devil woman
   I already hate myself in the mornings—
That ain't gonna change.

She tasted like coffin dust and rose petals
had the shakes of the snakes in Congo Square
when she touched me I felt a bleeding
a puncturing in my palms and eyes
   Walk straight to the Mississippi
   Don't speak, don't touch no one, you hear?

I tasted like last chances and bitters
had the chills of a woman half-past her death
when I touched her I felt a passing
a soft whisper in the space between my ears
   Everyone who'd listen to me is dead
   I got nothing but the river to look forward to
   But I'll be back missus, I'll show 'em all then

Because I'm Stained Red

My bathtub is filled with blood
and I'm not sure how that's possible
because I don't have a drain
but the red is beckoning,
and my clothes are falling off,
collecting in small piles as I move
from my bedroom to the hallway

and I can't remember a time when my life
wasn't red, wasn't ripped open and dripping messages,
screaming at me to stitch it back together again

because Dad told me it would get easier
when he found me at 19 covered in bruises and piss,
soaked in fear with my nails in my calves,
but my bathtub is still blood
and I'm still soaking in it, stained red,
stained suicide, I don't think
I'll ever be clean.

Becoming a Pyromaniac After Learning What the Word Meant

There was a book that I read in seventh grade about a boy who set barns on fire. I never looked at fire as anything but something my father built when the weather got cold and our house started to shake, but this boy and his barns made destruction look beautiful, and I was out of ways to hurt myself.

After school one day, I came home and went to the kitchen sink. I took the towels off the rack, stuffed them down the drain. They blossomed like paper lilies, lilies I set on fire with the matches I stole from the outside garage.

And I liked it.

So I set my room on fire, burned a hole through the carpet on our living room floor. In high school, I used to sit on the roof and smoke, throw cigarettes on the ground to see if they'd ignite. When I got to college, I collected all my journals, my diaries that I'd written in since I was eight years old. I doused them in gasoline, torched my memories and my words until they were nothing but ash.

And I liked it.

Because ash was final. Ash was empty. Ash was void. My past crumbled between my fingers, disappeared in the way the Autumn wind blew through my hair. Ash gave me control. It let me say goodbye to moments I wish I never said hello to, and now when I see a barn, I smile knowing that I no longer have to burn it down.

Before Leaving Ireland, Summer of 2015

We always saw morning,
early hours, but never sun rise,
and yet I've woken to this palette every day
aware and forgiven
my spirit still screaming,
and the sky here wears my bruises,
Jolene.

Beneath the Animals of Dark

A scratching near my ears lets me know about the fangs
in my neck, about the teeth in my jugular, and now, my body
numb to the curse that pumps through my veins, traumatized
by the pallor of the stars that light the forest floor, I lick
my wounds and crawl back to the tent, the afterbite of the
animals of dark sinking into my dreams, telling me about
mothers and moons, about imprisonment and change as
I wake two hours later to the sound of bones breaking
against the howling of my new night.

Beware the Witch Bottle in My Kitchen

It's easy, really. Magic. All you have to do is want something bad enough,
so bad that you're not afraid to take it, that you're not afraid of consequence,
of reaction. If your intention is tainted, then you're acting on poor faith, and
poor faith breeds bad energy, curses, blasphemy. Read your anger. Listen to
what it says.

Now pick up the vial.
    Whisper your desire inside of it.

Add a sprinkle of rosemary for good memories, a dash of sage to purify
what's bad. Fill the bottle with blades, with anything that can cut, stab, or
    wound; I've
used nails and staples, screws and paperclips. I entwine them, I release them,
    with my words
I cut through negativity, I sever the abuse.

    Now fill the vial with wine.
    Cork it alongside your tears.

Light a red candle and drip the wax over the seal, say your wishes,
recite your dreams. When I pray, I cry, and that intensifies my intent,
my purpose. I'm not a witch, but I'm not just a girl, and when the flame
touches me, I hardly feel it anymore.

Breaking Glass on the Way to Accidentally Falling in Love

We were lost somewhere in Ohio and it was dark and our phones were dead but we'd stocked my car with bad decisions and booze even though we were already late and a little bit drunk. He offered me a beer, offered me his lips, and I drank them both while I drove us down back country roads, telling ghost stories I didn't know the ending to while I watched him watching me trying hard not to show how happy I was because

> it was easy, too easy, and we drank ourselves drunk and got lost in the words thinking that if we threw the bottles out the car window that no one would ever know, that if we hit a tree, we'd get extra points, that if we ended up dead in the fog that surrounded the car, it would be almost too perfect, that if we fell in love by the end of the weekend, we wouldn't have to tell anyone, including ourselves:
>
> especially ourselves.

Burial Instructions to Hide the Body

The graveyard air tasted acrid, wet,
like the stale press of funerary petals on my tongue
melting alongside saliva
while I stood there pacing,
while I stood there praying,
knowing that we would never meet again,
that I was on this side of the death gate
for a reason, my stone unmarked,
my soul forgotten, my body buried
away from you for its own protection.

Camera on the Dashboard, Body in the Trunk

My shoes covered the passenger seat as I flew barefoot down I-75,
a line of coke settling somewhere in my sinuses
as I screamed out the driver-side window,
rain in my hair, music turned up to somewhere near almost-deaf

An empty bottle of Tequila rolled out from under my seat,
a half-pack of cigarettes lodged itself tight in my back pocket
as I fumbled for the business card of the gentleman
I was to meet at Love's gas station at 2:15 a.m.

They couldn't scream, but I imagined they tried,
a dishrag stuffed into their mouths, Duct Tape stretched across
taut flesh as I handcuffed them together in the trunk, bound
their hands and feet so they couldn't push out the taillights.

I parked the car to the side by itself, got out and tapped twice on the trunk
a small silver car, one big enough to hold a secret, let out a sigh
as I walked into the gas station, ordered a coffee, left the keys on the
counter along with a polaroid and then hitchhiked my way home.

Cancel the Reservations

The lamp on the table of our $65.00-dollar room wouldn't turn off
He sat there on the bed watching infomercials in his underwear
I didn't like the way the bathroom smelled because of the bodies in the tub
    Miss, there's been a noise complaint. Is everything okay?

The comforter was stained and didn't match the pillowcases
His boots were scuffed and covered in mud, bits of gravel lodged into the soles.
My shirt was ripped at the shoulder—bitch damned near pulled the whole thing a part.
    Miss, I'm going to need you to calm down.

The knife rested in the ice bucket as it cleaned itself non-guilty
His right hand moved against his cock as he jacked off to the woman selling jewelry
I couldn't get the sweat knots out of my hair.
    Miss, if you keep screaming I'm going to have to call the cops.

The shower ran cold against the red-spattered walls
He threw our stuff into a bag and locked the front door
I put on my jacket, climbed out the window, dropped 10 feet down, twisted my ankle
    Miss? Hello? Are you there? We're sending someone up.

Catcalling at the Devil in Sin City

It was morning and I felt the aftertaste
of memory on my tongue. I chugged moonshine
out of a plastic cup, ran out on the strip to where the sun
burned into my corpse-shined skin
as I blushed in Sin City next to a man
who held a sign that said:

    THE DEVIL IS HERE
    DON'T GIVE ME MONEY
    GIVE ME BOOZE

And there I was, half-drunk and reeling after
a one-night stand with my demons who went in dry. I asked him
if he knew where the devil was, but he called me crazy;
I laughed and handed him a 10, sat next to him and flipped his sign,
wrote my own message on the back in my lipstick

    GIVE ME MONEY
    GIVE ME BOOZE
    FUCK THE DEVIL

We got drunk until the morning sun
cooked me poisoned, yelled at strangers about the secret things
they did in the dark, cried about the public shame
we both felt about losing faith in people, in God;
I left the strip at sundown, hell in my back pocket,
a summer burn on my shoulders, but I had money
and I had booze and it felt good to be the sinner.

Chase the Morning with a Spoonful of Failure

Sunrise, the thoughts were pounding in my head,
a steady *drum drum drum* that beat incessantly
into the idea of morning, into the notion of another day

   Someone make me coffee
   Someone slit my throat

Light poured in between the blinds, little rays
of delicate poison that pricked my skin, bloodied my eyes,
reminded me that I was cursed, a dying black cloud

   Someone feed the dog
   Someone dig my grave

Daytime, the clock that shaved off minutes, years,
A fucking *tick tick tick* that reminded me of loss,
of the reality that I was dying here every day alone.

   Someone get me a job
   Someone bury me alive

Crossroads Are for Lovers Who Aren't Yet Enemies

Twenty-three with a drinking habit and nowhere to go,
I drove the roads with an urgency, a fuck-all attitude
before I stopped in the town that had already given me scars,
that had already pushed the razor against my teeth, and I shot
whiskey with my roommate, turned down a sure thing at the bar,
did yoga in one of my old college buildings before
I got the courage to go back and pick up the guy
I had my eyes on for the past five years,

      and the bar was closing and my mouth was dry and I dripped
      fear like the perfume I spilled earlier that evening, and yet I asked
      for his name, like I didn't already know, like I hadn't yearned for him
      to speak to me for years, and he smiled and laughed and whispered
      my name back to me, and in Poland, we say *swój ciągnie do swojego*:
      and our gypsy hearts recognized each other immediately,
      talking skulls, talking charms, sharing stories, sharing laughs.

There were back alleys and Walmart parking lots and he slipped a ring
on my finger and I told him I was going to kiss him and he was the first
boy I kissed who smiled the entire time our tongues danced, who held
my face instead of my breasts, instead of my hips, and we slept that night in
a hotel room with the blankets over our faces, with our noses touching,
and our black hair braiding together.

      and in Poland, we say *modli się pod figurą a diabła ma za skórą*
      and neither of us knew it then, but the devil under our skins had no
      intention of leaving, no matter how much we prayed, no matter how much
      we tried, cried, and attempted to die, and in the morning, he kissed my hand
      and told me I was his perfect day, and four years later, the devil is still
      laughing at the life we tried to build.

David Bowie is Dead
Inspired by "Lazarus" from Blackstar

Heaven, such darkness
Lazarus wept in an empty wardrobe
Over scars the world would never see
   Set me free
   Set me free
She imagined a bluebird singing
under the bandages on her eyes
a man spoke to her of death
   I'm out of breath
   I'm out of breath
Hospitals, such ghostings
The room spun without gravity
Sprinkled stardust on her lips
   One more kiss
   One more kiss
She shook in the darkness
Arms outstretched to his voice
He tells her it will be okay
   Just slip away
   Just slip away

Default Black

My heart is the empty side of the bed. My voice,
the crack in his coffee cup. I wonder if my father
thought about me today. If my boyfriend,
the man who told me he wanted to marry me,
thought about my smile when the woman
from his hometown
made him laugh.

I swallow the memories of empty picture frames. My fingerprint,
his signature scribbled in a copy of his book. I wonder if my mother
regrets telling me I shouldn't have been born. If my best friend,
the girl who took my knife away,
cried when she decided that I wasn't her maid of honor,
that I could attend her wedding
but not stand by her side.

And my bones are the leaves covering my car. My whispers,
the broken glass from the mirror I broke. I wonder if my brother
wishes he would have stood up for me. If my last lover,
the only man I believed when he told me I was beautiful,
dreams about me when the seasons change
when the clouds get angry,
start to scream.

But there's this silence in my eyes. My footsteps,
the quiver in his final words. I wonder if God
hears my prayers in the shower anymore. If anyone,
a single person who's passed me on 5th Avenue
noticed I was even there, walking, existing,
begging for someone
to tell me that I was.

Departure

5:55 p.m. flight to Baltimore
I've cried twice since I've been at the airport
The bartender brings me a double shot of jack, straight up,
    Keep them coming.
    I'm drowning.

Five minutes till boarding
I wasn't supposed to be here like this
My phone rings and that makes it worse
    Shoot the whiskey.
    I'm dying.

He hands me my receipt
Gives me a napkin to wipe the mascara off my face
I give him my signature, he gives me a free shot
    Swallow the burn.
    I'm flying.

Desperate Choices

The silence of my casket
resonates
with the feeling
in my heart

because I'm going to quit my job today
because I'm going to leave my family
because I'm going to leave my home

and

the quietness of my spirit
envelops
the words stuck
in my throat

because I'm never coming back
because I'm never apologizing
because I'm never feeling like this again

and

the numbness of my escape
spreads
in the hollow
of my chest

because I'm choosing to fight
because I'm choosing to grow
because I'm choosing to heal

and

the stillness of my mind
settles
in the calm
of my hands

because it's over
because it's over
because it's over

Driving the Road to Nowhere Fast

Ten hours into the drive, ganja on my breath,
tequila in my coffee cup, I'm running, I'm driving,
an escape from the howlings, from the screamings
of days and nights where I slept with gravediggers
and felons, spent the night in prison for an accident
no one believed, my shirt ripped, my shoes muddied,
tears in my jeans the size of the plot holes in my story

A stranger shook me awake on 376 with
dirt under his nails, with blood on my cheek,
but the gasoline helped with that—scrubbed it right off—
and it made my hair shine while masking the stench
of corpse, of rot, of last calls and death-bed promises
that will burn me alive, ignite me in sleep if insomnia
doesn't beat me to death first.

The steering wheel is talking but I stopped listening
years ago. I close my eyes when I drive, let the hallucinations
tell me where to go, how fast to get there, and sometimes
when it's cold out, I'll pick up a passenger on my way
to Cincinnati, sing him some songs about the ghosts
in the trunk, and if he makes it through the night,
I'll buy him breakfast at the truck stop,
kiss him good luck as I leave him stranded in the snow.

Energy Songs in a Texas Swamp

The road speaks if you listen to it,
tells you where to go, whispers how to get there—

It took me to the bayou once, once when I was alone in Texas,
when it fed me my habit of dangerous situations as I pulled off the road,
went down a dirt path, found a picnic table with a chain attached it,
a single shoe off to the side.

And the gravel yells if you trespass
screams when you go too far, too fast—

I took my sandals off, walked in the water
deep enough to get me wet with mud, damp with algae and leaves,
but there I was, dressed in a black sundress
standing in the swamp, the gray hair of the widow
swinging in the trees like moss, like webs.

And the earth chants if it feels one of its own,
protects the ground when it knows I'm there—

The storm came then, a howl of wind that blew
The table over, that sent the chains rattling, the shoe dancing across
the woods. I bent down to feel the electric, to feel the hymn of
curse, and it kissed my hand in a marsh that turned red, that turned
my dress crimson, that told me it was time to leave.

Emergency Masturbation Fantasy

I masturbate to an empty chair
my hand moving up and down
like yours never did
   I try to see your face
   Scream your name
But   I   can't

And I wonder if you exist
if my memories are from photographs of people I never met
whose stories I don't know
   I climax to your eyes
   Taste the saliva on your lips
But   I   don't

Because you're an empty chair
and my box is broken
like yours never was
   I should stop blaming myself
   Quit bleeding for sport
But   I   won't.

Escaping the Forest, I Found My Voice

The woods are still quiet with his voice. I think about the time
I left him there, abandoned him on the side of the road. He walked away
after kicking my car, told me he'd "see me around,"
but he wouldn't, not after the things I'd done.

Sometimes I lie to myself about it. I tell myself
I cried on the way home, but the truth of it
was that it felt good leaving him there,
alone, cold, my gray blanket on the forest floor
covered in rain, in fear.

When I touch the trees, I can remember his screams,
how he told me he liked me better on drugs. I was faster then,
happier when I couldn't slow the world down. He'd sing me
Jack White songs, tell me I deserved better. That
was supposed to make me forget the bruises, make
me forget the night I almost called the cops.

The first time he pushed me, I stayed down. The second time,
I grabbed him by the throat, told him to think twice
about what he was doing. My father would have been proud.
my brother would have killed him. I don't know
what I would have done. But I didn't run. And when I did leave,
I didn't look back.

I just kept driving. No matter how loud
the ground wept.

Exit Wounds in His Kiss, Your Memory

I didn't know what to expect when he leaned in and kissed me,
when the smell of coconuts and cologne entwined themselves
in my hair, but there we were, panting and breathless, a Tom Waits
record playing in the background while we smiled into each other's
skin and tried to forget the people who broke our hearts, and in some
ways it was easy, easy because of the jazz, because of the rasp in his voice,
and when my shirt came off, I shook his hair from its bun, playfully bit his lip,
my body eager, his body ready, and we fell into each other without
hesitation, without second guessing, even though the ghost of my heart
still lingered on this couch, this couch where I told you I loved you,
where I slept with my robe open and your hands between my legs, but
now it's him who's touching me and it's your face that's fading and
I don't know what I feel other than shame and orgasm, other than
guilt and electric, but the ghosts are screaming louder, and their yells
are getting closer and it hurts, and it hurts, this memory of you, and
sometimes I wish our story would erase itself, that I could hit delete
on eight months back, but your name on my tongue keeps me
strong when he falls asleep with his arms around me, when he kisses
me good morning and brings me coffee before I go to work, because
I refuse to believe that my heart has died, and when it rains, I put on
our old song and teach him something about love that I used to know
and you used to like.

Extracting Ectoplasm from Freshly Dug Corpses

The job wasn't hard, maybe physically if you stopped long enough to notice, maybe emotionally if you took a moment to breathe and think about what you were doing, but for me, it was just a gig, just something to pay the ghosts with so they'd keep working, so they'd keep searching—*do you hear me, Jolene? Are you listening?* —but no matter how many bodies I delivered, no matter how many vials filled, she still came to me at night, visited me in my dreams, gave me visions and slipped me hallucinations that were painful enough to make me stab out my eyes, but still my sight remained, even from behind my father's black bandana, and when I'd jump in their graves, feel their bones against my skin, I'd hear them pleading at me not to rob them, begging for me to let their spirit find peace, but the fire in my mind that burned with his face made me rip out their death, siphon it through my lips, and I sucked, and I sucked, my mouth against theirs until prior versions of the people they used to be dribbled down my chin and into the necklace that swayed near the resting place of my heart, and at night when I'd sleep in their coffins, sometimes I'd see his soul burning, his limbs dismembered, his eyes ablaze, and I'd smile because that's how Jolene said *thank you*; that's how she rocked me to sleep while the others went to work.

Filleting My Body for Old Time's Sake

I have a knife I keep in a wooden box in my room. It's next to a picture of a memory I made when I was sixteen years old in the basement of my parent's house with the boy I thought I would marry. We had ice water and coffee and he would take a sip of the hot, of the cold, and then kiss me on some part of my body to see how I would react. He told me he wanted my sixteen to be sweet, so he took icing from my cake and traced my lips pink so he could watch me lick it off.

> I was in my softball uniform then, high socks and covered in dirt. He told me I looked the most beautiful when I was coming down from a fight, when I was covered in bruises from trying to protect something, and I laughed at him because he was sweaty from basketball practice and his lip was busted, both of us bloody and now covered with cake and sex.

I don't celebrate my birthday anymore since he went away, and if I do, I celebrate it with my blade, with my wrist—my favorite place to be kissed—and sometimes when I think of him, I dig a little harder, but not because he's gone, but because I lost that version of myself when he walked away, that part of me that believed in moments that were worth keeping, memories that were worth making, futures that were worth planning.

Forcing My Ghost on Monastery Grounds

Ripped like my favorite pair of black stockings,
I crumble, a severing in these Dublin nights.
There's a blank line on my gravestone
that calls for signature, for commitment
yet I cry with the gulls that fly above these sepulchers,
My left hand naked after swallowing
the engagement ring you bought for me
seven months ago.

And everywhere there's a silence,
A harkened scowl etched in the wind;
I stumble over open plots and dead bouquets
Hear your whisper on my neck
While thoughts of you slip between
the earth blanket I've wrapped myself in
six feet deep, buried down dark and alone.

So hear me, sweet willow that dances before my
Weary eyes. Protect me while I choke and sleep,
Keep my prayers close, and my cries screaming;
I want this city to hear me weep long after I've
Said my goodbyes.

Forgetting How to Form New Memories

Quiet moments with rain and clouds, the simple pleasure of fresh coffee and someone's smile buried in my hair; I woke with dust in my lungs, unable to breathe for so long, but he kissed my lips wet, positioned himself against the small of my back, and in my head, I heard Patti Smith singing "Cartwheels" as I adjusted my see-through tank top so the side of my breasts could be seen out of the corner of his eye.

> The frigid still of the summer breeze crept in through the window, snuck between my legs where he rested his hand, afraid to move up, desperate to move down but the tension between the deaths of our hearts overwrought the call of our sex.

And these strangers in the room with us, these hallucinations and holograms of projected emotions, watched us as we wilted into each other's arms trying to find the part of ourselves that we gave away, that we surrendered without knowing; I try to see him, try to pretend that he's enough to keep me distanced from the hole that deepens in the crevice of my still present-past, but when he looks at me, I can't remember his name because on my tongue, I'm still wrestling to get away from the taste of yours.

Full Dark, Only Black

The roads were slick and the cigarette that burned in my bra
almost made me wreck, but I left it there because I hoped the
potential scar might remind me to stop driving at 4 a.m.
might force me to stop sleeping across states in back alleys
and motel lots where men and women sneak out of each other's rooms,
drive away drunk like nothing happened, like nothing mattered

and maybe it didn't, maybe it doesn't, but I still keep a blanket
in the backseat of my Fiesta and I still look for potential places
to sleep when I'm driving, and full dark, only black, that was
the state of my mind and the description of my nights, my time
on the road with a bottle of whiskey stashed in my glove compartment
and a supply of cigarettes stashed between the seats

because I needed something when it got too quiet, something strong
when the memories and the panic started to settle with me
at rest stops and near guardrails and in parking lots and
gas station restrooms. My hands still shake when I touch the steering
wheel, tremble a bit when I take out my keys. I wonder if I'll
stop thinking of driving to you, if there will be a time when I
let myself travel without the familiarity of your name on my tongue,
if someday, the desire to get in my car at all will finally go away.

Funeral in August of 2016

For James

The sun was out, but she was drowning
by the dam I won a fishing contest at
when I was eight.

    The kids who found her didn't win anything,
    just memories of a floating corpse,
    of a suicide gone right.

A family with too much tragedy
for it to be a coincidence,
we stood in her garden together.

    I held my cousin's hand knowing he
    couldn't understand. We danced near roses
    while he asked me where 'mom' was.

Give Me a Reason to Sing

I wrote sheet music to the way he looked at me that morning, typed up songs to the night we drank beer and fucked in his bedroom, but the notes dropped off the page and the lyrics erased from the paper, and with each chorus and every title, my nightmare kept getting darker, kept getting sharper, sharper like knives, like words, like too-focused pictures of me that sit in a computer file unopened for months, and if I try to remember the tune, try to siphon the words, everything goes black, black like tar, black like minor notes, black like my eyes when I forget the taste of his voice,

> because this musician wears the essence of our time together etched into her fingers and her eyes, has sold her likeness at the crossroads two-times over to a man with a promise and a full head of dark hair, and sometimes when I sit at home and play piano, when I lay in bed and strum guitar, I think of how I'm burning in another life, how I'm ripped apart and living this world in pieces, and when the time comes for the man to collect payment, when the moment arrives where I have to pay my debts, I'll carve your name on my tongue so when I sing in Hell every drop of blood is in your memory, every song still only sung for you.

Go Set the Ghosts to Possession

Teenage-me wanted to touch the ghosts inside her, wanted to close her eyes and talk to the monsters that woke her up in the middle of the night, that fed her daydreams during her high school hours, that held her hand when she ran away from home, so she went to a castle in Brownsville, spent her evenings playing with spirits in the courtyard, her nights telling stories in the nursey, her mornings reading poems in the master bedroom. Sometimes she slept where the Bowman's held wakes, rifled through old grocery lists and dressed up in vintage clothes, and sometimes she couldn't keep her candles lit, or help the cold from setting in because

>one night, there was a séance and she was leading it, a conduit for the dead with her arms open, her mind willing, and she called to them, those who had died where she stood, where she'd fallen asleep to reruns of *Grey's Anatomy*, where she'd called her dad at 3 a.m. telling him that there was something sitting in this house with her,

>and that's when another's breathing started in her chest, when a voice whispered in her ears and shook the gooseflesh from her skin. When she felt the man reach up through her throat, she screamed to break the connection, felt him slide out through her back in a short life, a quick death, and she ran out of that room, out of that castle, blessing herself and praying to gods, and at night when she thinks of ghosts, she remembers the way hers almost crawled out of her, and she pulls the covers tighter, anxious to keep them in.

Grabbing for Cigarettes, Grabbing for Teeth

Smoking down 51, on fire, on speed, I listened to the songs
that first made me want to run, that told me to hide, that I was
being followed, that she was with me again, so I lit my
dreamcatcher on fire, put out the flame on my arm, and
in my pocket, there were teeth for the toll, for the price
I had to pay for still being alive, and with every life I took,
with every smile I broke, it slashed away at morals,
at the core death I always wore, and I became stronger
so I could keep going, so I could escape her just once,
just once so I could pull over and finally take a break.

Gravity Glue for Chakra Health

For Stephen

Stacking rocks against the movement of the river,
the water past my ankles, like cold, like ice
I focused on gravity, thought about symmetry
while you found broken beer bottles, collected pastel
shards that made my summer brighter, somehow more alive,
and with my hands, I meditated, aligned myself with the
ebb and flow of the breaks against my feet, feeling for the first
time that I could do this, that I could finally let myself breathe,
let myself shut down, somehow glue my chakras back together.

Guitar Players Wear Pain Like I Wear Stilettos

When you've killed a man like I have, when you've walked away with his blood on your hands, it's no wonder why notes turn into tears, why songs turn into wounds, and my stilettos remind me of the knife, of the cuts and the stabs that I gave, and now I walk on glass, on nails, on blades to remind me that I'm weak even when I think I'm strong, and there's something that connects me to the sound of the guitar, to the slide of the strings, to the ache of the strum, and when I'm on break from Death, I like to listen to the men who play me my favorite songs, who remind me of the first time I fell in love, who take me back to the nights I screamed in his bed, to the mornings I yelled in my car, to the boy who fucked me in cemeteries, and to the man who accidently made love to me in hotel rooms.

> Yes, I'm a sucker for an artist, for a guitar player who wears pain on his face, and that kind of sadness makes me feel safe because it's the makeup that I put on each day before I go to work, each night before I cry myself to sleep, and there's no wonder why I dream of nights that sing, why I fantasize about a man who can show me how to survive, who can play me a song that makes me want to stop running, stop hiding, stop burying myself down deep, but the night doesn't have time for women who like to write music, so I leave the bar and the tab that I've been running for four years, kiss my sorrowful muse goodbye as Death waits at the door. I'll be back after I collect more bodies, and maybe next time, my sweet cowboy, the song will be on me.

Hanging Imaginary Drapes in Jefferson Hospital

For Nana—I love you.

At 85, hospital rooms looked like home—
my grandmother, deep into dementia, with tubes in her
nose, needles in her arm, grabbed at the air and yelled at me
to fold the invisible blankets, to hang the imaginary drapes,
and my father sat in the corner staring at me while my mother
wept into a pillow on the other side of the bed, but I kept pretending,
kept trying to help clean my Nana's room, and when the doctors
held her down to put in her catheter, I held her hand while she cried,
while she looked at me and said *you shouldn't have to watch your grandmother die*,
and when my brother came in, she smiled at the handsome stranger,
grabbed my shirt and asked me who he was.

Head Ornaments

The wind tousled her hair,
rocked her skull back and forth;
she hung there, a tree ornament
as one end of the rope dressed the branch, the other, her neck;
black eyes, night eyes, stared into the forest, into the snow,
her death cutting through ice
while she searched for her torso,
scanned the ground for her limbs,
but he had taken them,
whisked them away from this burning white hell,
from this frozen inferno,
and he had left her here,
here, suspended and alone,
left only to sway in the chill,
to dance amongst the snowflakes and ash,
a hypnotic pendant dressed in flesh,
a bleeding orb locked in permanent scream.

Hitchhiking to Stop the Voices

He pulled off the road, window down, a blunt between his lips,
I didn't say anything, just walked up to the car and got in the backseat
and we drove in silence while I reapplied my lipstick, changed my clothes,
but he never turned the radio on and I hated when the world went silent,

because when the world went silent, I had too much time to think,
and there were headphones in my pocket, but he wouldn't let me use them
and I didn't ask a second time, just untangled the cords, smoothed
them out against the bare flesh of my thighs while I stared at the chapped
indents on my wrists and ankles

because when the world went silent, the memories started to come back,
and I didn't say anything, and he didn't recognize me, so I slipped the cords
around his neck, watched him kick, watched him struggle, watched him die
before I opened the door, shoved his body out, smiling at the sound it made
when it hit the side of the road,

because when the world went silent, I was forced to relive it,
to go through the torture all over again, so I turned the music on,
tossed my headphones out the window, and with AC/DC screaming
and another death on my hands, the voices went away for a bit,
and I had plenty of time to find my next dose of medicine,
thumb out and willing somewhere down the road.

How the 80s Taught Me About Trauma Bonding

His hair was longer than mine, curly like Bon Jovi's was in the 80s and he looked like Steven Tyler, lips big and wet, and I bet that *pink was his favorite color* while we sat there talking in Polish, him telling me how he had to wear makeup around his one eye because his girlfriend got mad and hit him, me sitting there at the bar dripping while my ex played the songs he wrote for me at an open mic he and I still went to every Wednesday night.

"You're still in love with him," Steven Tyler said.
"No, I'm not. I just can't stay away from him. There's a difference."

I'd been driving to Greensburg and sleeping in my car just to be next to him for a few hours all summer, but he didn't notice how much he still loved me until the rock star impersonator kissed me in the parking lot and pulled my hair in a haze of smoke. I can still remember his face when he saw us, how he came up to me and said he was leaving, leaving without me, in spite of me, because of me. I begged him not to, told him we could build a fire in the woods, told him that I'd find him in the mountains later on, but that was the beginning of the disappearing.

"No girl drives all this way just for an ex," Bon Jovi said.
"I'd drive states for him without giving it a second thought."

We saw each other one more time after that where I apologized and screamed with my eyes that I was still in love with him, but I kept my mouth on the Sam Adams I was drinking while I sat there watching him watching me, both of us knowing that the trauma bond between us was too strong, the breaks too fresh, the cuts not yet healed, but neither of us knowing how to say goodbye again because we couldn't do it the first time, because leaving was its own injury, because we'd cut holes into places were only the other could fit.

"Those songs he used to play up there. Were they about you?" Steven Tyler said.
"Yeah. At one time or another, I think they all were."

Hunted Down from the Other Side

In an antique store on Route 19, a dead girl grabbed my hand,
told me to buy her portrait and hang it next to the photograph
I found at a yard sale of two Romanian children, the one that
unnerved my father, that made him beg me to give it back, but
also next to the dead solider and the young married couple
I found captured in a trunk somewhere off Route 40 buried
beneath wake notes and death certificates, dirt and dried flowers.

Her voice was big, nagging, and she wore a black petticoat with
white stockings and glossed-over shoes. She tugged on my
shirt pocket and asked me where I lived, how long it would
take before she was settled into her new home, and I told her
to watch her tone and keep her manners or the other ghosts
who kept watch over me wouldn't care for her much.

> She was quiet then, nervous-like, but I cleared off the passenger seat,
> let her ride up front with me so she could see the new world,
> could see what she was getting herself into, and off my mirror hung
> a dreamcatcher, off my dashboard, an evil eye, and I could see she
> was getting nervous, curious-like, but still afraid. *Little girl*, I spoke,
> *Little Madeline, what made you ask me to be your mom?*

She twisted the buttons off her jacket, pulled at the corners
of her hair. Her big brown eyes somehow got bigger as she
recognized the sound of her name, and when she reached
into her coat pocket, she pulled out a gold hunter's compass,
set it in my lap. *I found this on the other side. A man told me
it was yours, that you needed it so you could get back home.*

And I cried then because the last time I saw that piece
was when I handed it to the man I loved, a man who died
time and time again, who never showed up in pictures,

who never reached out to me because my men and women,
my children and my sibling kept him hidden, kept him shrouded,
kept him dead and still, locked up and silent.

    I was quiet then, nervous-like, but I stepped on the gas,
focused on the road so I could drive back to safety, hang her
next to the others, next to Caleb and Jezebel, Matthew, Ronald
and Jessica, and she could see I was getting nervous, curious-like,
but still afraid. *Mommy,* she said, *don't be mad at me, but he
said to hurry, hurry before he kills us, all of us. Do you know
how to get home now? He said he wants to see you try.*

I Am Not Your Daughter

The first time I gagged sucking cock,
I cried; my breath—
caught somewhere between my lungs
and my uvula—stopped
when the man,
the man who rammed my head down
harder
and
harder,
asked me
to call him
Daddy.

I remember wiping my mouth,
disgusted, filthy; my hands—
frozen somewhere between my morals
and my pride—shook
when the man,
the man who asked me to spread my legs
wider
and
wider,
called me
his bitch
and told me
to beg.

I Build Versions of You That Won't Leave

I wait here, in the catacombs of my mind, resurrecting bodies that remind me of yours. I pick up skulls, run my tongue against their teeth, and I think about the time you made me come on your couch while I wore my black baby doll dress. There was champagne on the table, lipstick on your throat, and my hands were wet from the sweat that trailed down your back.

I don't know whose bones these are,
but I remove two teeth from the skull
and tuck them into the pocket of my skirt
so I can remember how you taste.

Yes, there are torches on my synapses and I pick up femurs that remind me of your legs. If I close my eyes, I can still see you standing there fucking me while I'm bent over your bed, both of us in our robes while breakfast burned on the stove downstairs. To my left are the pelvic bones, to my right, are the spines, and I think about you twisted in orgasm while you made love to me in the shower, the scent of her shampoo in the air.

I don't know who they belong to,
but I take one of each
and tuck them into the bag across my shoulder
so I can remember how you stood.

And there are cobwebs in my cortex as I rebuild your skeleton. Time and time again, I make versions of you that won't walk away while I come here to let myself be human, to allow myself to feel, and when I see the outline of your body, see the subtle smile that used to pepper your face, I lie down and wait for you to tell me you're back, that this time you're not going away, but the torches go out, and the catacombs grow still and somewhere deep down, I know you'll always be gone.

In a Name, There are Ten Thousand Lies

It's easy to erase something that never existed:
like smoke, like flame, it
   suffocates, disappears in air,
     extinguished, gone.

Iron and Silver Accent Her Life

You'll never see her wear gold; she doesn't like the way it looks against her skin,
against her porcelain paste, so there's always silver, a glittering of lustrous metal,
precious in its protection of her beauty and her throat. Cultivating a psychic connection
of purity to moon, she walks with enchantment keeping the undead at bay, a horseshoe
of iron on her barn, a trail of brick dust near her door.

There's a legend that she's a seer, a woman widowed too young
to come back from the pain, and now if you listen close enough,
you can hear her wail at night, screaming for the one
they took away. Some say he visits her when it gets dark,
that he stands at the foot of her bed, his neck snapped and hanging to the side,
the noose trailing behind him as he begs her to join him, to leave this world behind.
No one knows if this is true, but in the morning, she runs to the well in her backyard,
her long, dark hair swinging at the base of her back. She lowers the bucket, mutters her prayers,
her daily sermons, and bathes in the water of the world below, laughing as she dances
in the salt ring around her.

No, you'll never see her wear gold; it doesn't give her the security she needs,
the defense against the here and now that she requires, and in her sanctuary of crosses and nails,
she'll wear her charms and bless her medallions because there's no rest when you're cursed,
when the night burns you like you're still attached to the stake, and when you're living
in between the veil, a natural witch with too much knowledge, you do what you can to survive.

It's Raining in February and I Can't Find God

Wrapped in a blanket, I walked outside to the parking lot and sat down in the rain. I didn't move and I barely breathed. I just sat there, crying with the sky. The stars weren't out, but I repeated the *Our Father* over and over again, crying harder when I asked Him to pray for the hour of my death. Was this my hour? Was this my death? Would I die before 30 like I always thought I would? I used to write letters to God in my diary, but he never wrote back. When I got older, I'd write him notes on my arms, in the creases of my legs, but he just let me bleed.

And tonight, February wept harder, and I grew colder. It was winter and my face was numb. And yet I stayed out there, praying hard like the sinner I was, and I begged and begged for death, but still, I couldn't find God.

Jail Time for Harboring a Fugitive

One foot out the door, the other inside the cell
I held the bars with hesitation, unsure of where I felt safer,
which hand I should play. In my palm was a wanted man,
a Russian-Roulette game of life or death, and sometimes I won,
sometimes I didn't, but I've never been good at betting

   my poker face always gave me away

and in my pocket was a bullet and a guitar pic, last night's
underwear and change for tomorrow's coffee, and I could hear
you outside paying my fines, paying my debts, and all I wanted
was a shot of Tequila and the joint I rolled when they picked me up,
but the warrant for his arrest was on the wall, and he was still out there,
still laughing, still hiding, and I've never been good at leaving

   I always tended to come back

so I fell deeper into my jean jacket, shut off my tears,
buried my anxiety somewhere deep inside my chest. I walked outside,
the heels of my black boots clicking against the concrete floor,
and you smiled at me with a busted lip, and I nodded thanks
while the officer held the door open, warned me against going home,
about trying to fix someone who was always going to be broken.

Janis Joplin is My Spirit Animal Half-Past Dead

This was before I ripped my favorite black sweatshirt.
I was high in Wonderland, singing Russian gypsy music in my underwear.
He told me the world would stop spinning soon,
   but it gave me a reason to hold him, so I secretly hoped that it wouldn't.

This was before I knew how much I loved him.
I was shy then, but he took pictures of me because he thought I was beautiful.
He gave me his black hat, the one he was wearing when we first kissed
   Halloween night,
   said I looked like Janis Joplin, that my lips wrote music when he touched me.

This was before I let myself get lost again.
I was sitting on the couch, drinking orange juice and smoking a cigarette.
He reached out to me and took my hand, asked me to dance with him,
   told me that he would never hurt me, that with him, I was finally free.

Joyriding into the City We Burned Down

It was March and the streets were still full of ash,
ash from the night we arrived with gasoline,
with liquor bottles, with lighters. We had sex
on the hood of my car while they all screamed,
screamed as they burned alive, and I remember you
tucking a strand of hair into my braid,
telling me that you could see Hell in the reflection
of my eyes, telling me that if I wasn't careful, I'd burn
with them, too, but you were my laughter, my own
personal slaughter, and together we lit the city,
joyriding their deaths on the anniversary
of our favorite mass murder, cruising down the
highway to the memory of the first time we killed.

Just Let Me Go to Gone

I was in the walls already,
faded into the white like a letter
left in the sun too long, but you
kept writing me visible, kept
preserving what was left

—there was nothing left—

For I was part of the night already,
smudged into the darkness like a mistake
you couldn't erase, a shadow you kept
behind you, imprisoned, but always
at distance.

—all there was, was distance—

Because I was halfway to gone,
almost removed, practically deleted,
but you kept finding me, kept
bringing me back home, back to
the walls and the night, ever at
your mercy, always on your time.

—we were always out of time—

Just like the First Time I Caught Fire

I didn't put myself out
didn't scream, didn't cry;
I just stood there, smiled
   because after all the years,
they still thought
they could kill me.

Karma Tells Me What She Did to You

She is soft, always gentle
never pushes me away
just covers my eyes, shields
me from the blood, rocks me
to sleep with the lullabies
of murder stories, her serial kills

She is calm, always comforting
never blames me for her life,
just leaves me packages of limbs,
sends me notes signed with tears,
proof of what I've purchased
what I signed my name for,
what I've bought.

And she is beautiful, always smiling
never chastising me for being weak,
just an older sister who cleans up for me,
who takes care of my mistakes,
one hit, one shot, one cut,
to make it all go away, to bring
me peace when I wake up
after hearing about all their deaths.

Keg Stands and Car Accidents at Gunpoint

High school taught me about drinking,
about how to let boys put their hands on me,
fill me full of booze while my boyfriend
watched our classmate jump off the roof
while I was upside down

listening to drunks tell me stories about running away
about getting in car accidents and smashing mirrors
while my best friend grabbed my arm as the man
pulled out a gun, shot one of our friends

who told us to have an escape plan, to park
on the side of the road so when the cops got called
we could get away, and there's a scar on my hand
from when I dove into the rose bush, got cut up by
thorns so I wouldn't disappoint my parents
when they came to take us all away.

Key Places to Lose Your Blood

He walked me around and showed me all the places where people were killed, where people were tortured, where their throats were slit, their blood collected in buckets, their bodies dissolved in bathtubs, and I stood there holding his hand, thinking about how I'd been walking around this city alone for five drunken nights, and in front of the death houses he kissed my fingers and told me he could taste my energy, that the creatures that came out at night would surely eat me alive, that I should leave before he got hungry, that the vampires in this town were attracted to girls like me.

Killing Floor

It's routine now: the blood and the bleach. I can't see one without seeing the other, and my hands are stained white and red, my nose filled with the scent of copper and medicine. There's no more screams, no more shouts, and the silence is comforting like a glass of warm milk before bed and I can almost trace the outlines of their bodies as I count their corpses to fall asleep, stacking them on top of each other in my head as I drift away to the creaks of the floorboards as the dead try to escape.

Kneecaps for Lunch

Fifth Avenue stalking,
with three rivers to my left,
I walked the restaurant alleys,
touched the bridges
until I found him in a corner, sun-weathered,
starving, a paper bag of whiskey in his lap,
a yellow-stained newspaper two weeks past
over his arms and face.

I bent down to his level,
saw the wedding ring on his left hand,
but his shorts showed his kneecaps,
those circular wafers, those round bone cookies
that slipped and slapped when I poked them,
that rolled beneath my fingers
when I cut around the flesh.

Full of poison, he didn't notice,
didn't mind when I bit into his legs,
when I dissected my lunch, my dessert,
two little biscuits covered in red jam
I popped them in my mouth,
rolled them over my tongue,
still crunching and swallowing
when I walked into my office
later that afternoon.

Lanterns Hang at Feeding Time

Wrought iron lanterns
a pint of beer and a black baby grand,
a woman held the piano,
her voice, the crowd—
I stood there, taken, owned,
her black dress, its high slit,
the way she held
the cigar and the microphone
at the same time
much like how she held
the blood in the corner of her mouth
with no one noticing,
no one noticing,
except me,
me and the candlelight,
the marks on my neck.

Leftover Slaughter for Two

A pair of thighs and legs,
a set of breasts,
we wrapped them carefully,
packaged each piece individually
not wanting to leave anything behind,
not for fear of evidence,
but because we'd both been at this
long enough to know
that by the time we made it home,
we'd be ready to eat again.

Life, Interrupted

She smoked a joint on a stranger's back porch. It was good weed,
and she chased it with a pill she bummed off of the guy in the kitchen. On the
   outside
she looked normal, 25 and normal, but inside
she was tripping and flying and morphing and spinning.

The sky was too close
The trees were laughing skulls

It was Saturday and she didn't know where she was. There were
guns in the basement and she was drunk on champagne. That morning
there were panic attacks and screaming. She clutched her chest unable to
   breathe,
she smoked a cigarette to take her mind off the pain.

The walls were empty
The photographs were on fire.

She laid there topless with the cork in her hands, her hair
matted to her face, her mascara smeared. The world seemed smaller
without his hand to hold, without his voice in her head. She started to cry
but the stranger kissed her lips and told her to keep soaring

His floor was broken glass
His couch, an open grave

Like Smoke, Like Fog

The water dripped down in steady streams, in christening tears;
I cried for twenty minutes in the motel while the steam filled my lungs
with the leftover cries from my first heartbreak.
I wrote my name on the bathroom mirror
but I still can't see my reflection since he left.

Looking for the Headless Driver

After leaving my grandmother's house, my father would tell me about the headless driver who prowled Route 40 at night, looking for his long-lost passenger with brown hair and big dark eyes, and for years I searched for this driver, tried to flag him down on my way home from work, sat on guardrails to lure him my way, but months went by and years went by and when I found a dead man on the side of the road, his head missing, absent from the body bag, I knelt down and hugged his corpse, scrapped my elbow against the pavement, screamed about his homecoming as the police dragged me away.

Making Snow Angels Out of Songs of Madness

The heater in his car didn't work and my hands were burning but that didn't stop me from following him into the woods, from hiking into the forest in the middle of the night to find a treehouse, to make snow angels, to kiss under the moon in a clearing as big as the lies he told, as empty as the promises he made, and I remember how easy it was for me to believe this was going to be romantic, how sure I was that everything would be okay, and when he took my hand, he blew onto my fingers, kissed each one and told me he thought I would be prettier, that the other people didn't show up to kill me like he planned, and we laughed then, him hard, me uncertain, as he tackled me in the snow, like enemies, like lovers, and when we got home, he wrote me a song about being crazy, about how he was insane and I was dead, and when he sang it, he held up my book and kissed me, told me that no matter how bad it got, that he would always understand, that there wasn't anything I could do that could make him love me less.

Married to the Idea of My Death

I don't sleep in my bed,
but I stayed in it for two weeks, half-starved and dying
with a knife in one hand, my phone in the other

    while

        picture after picture, promise after promise
        my friends tried to find me, begged me to come back,
        to open my windows, to let them come save me

and I don't believe in God,
but I prayed every second of every day for just one reason
to keep breathing, one reason to have faith,

    while

        phone call after phone call, plea after plea,
        my father cried as he listened to me break,
        his voice quivering against the suicide in my voice

and I couldn't talk without screaming,
so I drank myself to sleep, to a world where my nightmares
were kinder than the life that I was given

    while

        knock after knock, email after email,
        my mother called just to hear me breathing,
        said my name to make sure it still sounded alive.

Memory Retrieval, 1991, Finleyville, PA

Our house scared me, but I remember Beauty and the Beast coming to one of my birthday parties; Mom and Dad brought in a castle and a cake, and I was a princess living in a fairytale except we were all still covered in the blood of our late-neighbor's death

> *And there's a curse in my passenger seat, a wish for those who hurt us, who cause us pain, inflict agony that can't be burned or cut away...*

And so the Devil grabbed us, licked our wounds and washed the blood from my hair; I was two, but I was branded with the mark of suicide—we all were—when Dad found George in the garage, gun in hand, skull in pieces as I held my E.T. doll and looked out the window, wondering what I could do to make my father laugh again

> *And there's this woman who stands behind me, a guide for when my life goes astray, who settles my scores and handles my bets so that I never have to be that scared girl again...*

But then Mom got pregnant and we fled the murder house, ran away and left the memories behind, but the darkness followed—*oh, did it follow*—and eight months later I was in a bathroom stall in the hospital, my mom on the floor covered in blood while my brother struggled for his life inside her, a premature miracle that I remember touching in the incubator, crying because I couldn't bring him home.

> *And there's this feeling I carry with me, an instinct for when the hurt becomes too much, that protects me when I'm weak, covers me when I'm vulnerable...*

But at 27, I don't work right anymore because there's too much blood inside me that's not my own, too much red on my hands from the nights I spent making tourniquets and bandaging wounds, too many scars left from my ex's bedroom four years ago when I found him cut up and crying on the staircase, and no matter how many times I paint my walls white, when I wake up, they're always red

> *Because there's this death that sits inside of me, whispering that it makes me stronger, that it makes me better, but deep down, both of us know I'm already spoken for, deep down both of us know I'm already in Hell.*

My Apologies, I'm Dead

Miss, are you ready to order?
I scanned the menu
Tried to remember my favorite
Dish.

I recommend a white wine to start.
I think I preferred
Red because it looked
Like blood

I'll give you a few moments.
I sat there staring,
Wondering how I got
here

Stephanie, did you decide?
I turned around,
Tried to figure out who
That was.

My Underwear Choice Wasn't for Him

Black makes me feel confident.
Lace makes me feel sexy. I wore them both
on my last night with him, and when we finished,
when my cell phone rang, when I told him I had to leave,
that he would always be special to me, that I was sorry,
he watched me get ready at the bathroom sink,
his eyes never leaving my profile.

I remember standing there, my underwear
half up my ass while I powdered my face
to take away the red. He asked if I wore those
underwear for him, if I was saving myself for
someone else, and we laughed
like old friends do.

I didn't feel regret, but his lips looked sad then,
and when he kissed me at the door, he said "I miss you already"
and I knew he really did. I think I would have loved him then,
then in that city, in that moment, in that room,
but my stilettos were digging into the carpet,
my alarm was going off, and all I could think about
was who I really put those underwear on for
and how on that day, it wasn't for him.

Naked in a Motel Room with Spilled Wine

My friend asked me to sleep with him the night I confessed to my lover that I wanted to fuck other people, and my pants were missing, and so was my shirt, and I had locked us outside the room by accident, but he had a knife, but he had a death wish, but he jumped off the balcony to get us back in, opened the door while he threw wine against the wall, broke the headboard, shattered the ash tray, and he told me I was a drunk, that he couldn't stand to look at me, so he slept outside, left me to wake up in my shawl wrapped with shame while he was in the shower, while he was in the car, and I was apologizing, and he was forgiving, and he slipped me some drugs when he kissed me at the stop sign, told me it would all be better soon, and when we got on the road, the colors were so bright that for a second, they actually were.

Navigating Family History

Grandfather said that our bloodline was tainted,
that there were secrets I couldn't know
like why we never talked about my uncle
or who was really buried in the family plot;

I didn't know our ancestry until my late twenties
had no idea about the meaning behind
the birthmark on my back, the one that's knotted,
hard like it's covering something,
something small, something silver;

Grandmother told me to stop asking questions,
that there were some things better left for dead,
dead like my uncle, like my aunt, like my cousin,
the harvest moon the last light they ever did see.

Near the Stairwell in the Dungeon

At the Dungeon on Bourbon Street,
I sat on the floor shaking,
trying to pick myself up.

My wounds weren't apparent yet,
but I knew I'd bleed out,
stain the city red with my curse.

I tried to look myself in the mirror
but the reflection that looked back
wasn't one that I knew.

I crawled to the bathroom
wrapped my arms around the toilet,
threw up the dirt I'd been buried beneath.

How foolish they were
to think they could make me disappear;
a wolf always finds her way back home.

Nocturnal Bee Song

With lips like sugar
I tongued my way inside her as she flew on cocaine, as she tripped on Molly;
my face covered with honey
the sound of her humming stuck in my throat
the sting of her venom sweeter with every drink.

Numb in April

We/ him and I/ used to talk about our suicide attempts
how we both flirted with death
but secretly wanted to live;
he cut his wrists the wrong way
I didn't take enough pills;
I came up for air in the bathtub
he checked himself into the hospital;

It was healthy, until it wasn't.

We cried a lot
when the sun went down;
sometimes, when it snowed,
I'd think about the ice in my lungs,
he'd tell me about the scars on his heart
and we'd sit there in his hand-me-down bed,
in his rented room in a drug house outside the city
kissing and making love to our sadness
while we drank in each other's company,
continued to die

And it was dark, until it went black.

I/ me and myself/ licked the barrel of a gun,
tasted the way it *could* have felt to have him stop breaking my heart;
to have the screaming stop,
the bruises go away, the blood stop dripping,
but I am/was weak in my strength;
I told him and he cried
he told me he was leaving

And it hurt—like hell—until it didn't.

Of My Wounds, There Are Many

Snapshot to blood and bone,
there's a knife in my head,
but my migraine was two years in the making,
stitched to the side of my skull
like the arrow tip lodged behind my eye,
buried in my brain like the bruises
of last night's thunder storm,
my teeth ripped from my mouth,
shoved down my throat
like how the sky pushes out rain.

Of my wounds, there are many:
see the delicate stigmata cut into my hands and feet,
the gashes dug into my thighs, the tally-mark slashes on my wrists;
I am the punctured female, the pincushion of hysteria,
a traumatized sack of feminine injury,
the flesh of my flesh, the scar of my scar,
I'm a collection of lesions and lacerations,
a patchwork of black and blue contusions
worn out from where you scrubbed me raw,
beat me till I seeped red like rare, woman steak.

Look to me on this table as I bleed and break,
a toy of operation, a surgical muse to the amputation
of bodily consciousness: hear me when I say I feel nothing,
that with each incision and penetration, I am dead,
gone from this world of torment and torture,
a disappearance, an acceptance to oblivion,
to the land where I can forget the flower,
the blossom of what I saw lies underneath.

Yes, use my soon-to-be-corpse as a nametag,

as a placard to the other girls who are destined to bleed;
I am closing my eyes to your knives now,
deafening myself to the fractures you inflict;
I will cease to be your canvas of mutilation,
Only a head, a torso, a heart,
best to photograph me while in transition;
it's the last chance you'll have
to locate my soul.

On Listening to "Dressed in Smoke" at 11:12 p.m.

This feeling is important so I'm going to write it down even though I'm throwing up while the cursor is blinking in front of me, even though I cried myself to sleep on the plane after reading your message, even though I drank all the wine in my apartment after looking at your letter and feeling like the pit inside my chest was never going to stop growing. I don't know what I'm preaching to myself these days, but the nightmare on my back that wears your face won't stop burying his claws into my shoulder blades. I can't close my eyes without seeing you on my couch kissing me, your hands buried in my hair while I said 'I love you' for the first time in person, and I can't dream without hearing you sing to me in the shower while you washed my hair in a peppermint and lavender haze.

> There's a record spinning in the corner of my living room
> it's playing to the tune of the collapse of my valves,
> to the melody of my fingertips typing this poem with blood

And this moment is important, so I'm going to be honest even though I've thrown away all of our memories but failed in erasing you from my heart, even though I still stay up till 4 a.m. but now it's from insomnia instead of our eight-hour conversations, even though after all this time when I say your name, part of my heart still tries to smile. I don't know what I'm doing day in and day out, but my poetry sings to the tune of the guitar song you never played for me and to the color scheme of the wedding we never got to plan. I can't get on the highway without counting down mile points in my head, can't sing to my favorite songs without seeing us dance in my kitchen, and when I cook, I imagine your hands around my waist, your breath on my neck, and it's hard to be afraid of monsters when the ghost of everything you haunts me with each passing moment.

> There's a clock ticking near the television
> it's counting down to the collapse of my chambers
> to the breaking of my bones trying to run from this hurt

But this moment is important, so I'm going to leave even though I spent months crying in bed begging God to bring you back, even though on my 27th birthday, I lit a single candle and wished for you when I blew it out, even though I flew halfway across the country to spend what should have been our anniversary, alone and writing poetry to the city lights we should have been making love to. I don't know how strong I am, but I haven't died yet despite the bleeding wound that I had to section off with a tourniquet. I can get up in the mornings now and look myself in the mirror, just like I can trick myself into happiness with the warmth of a stranger's touch and the brush of their lips against my cheek. But still, after all this time, when I laugh a little too hard, when I smile a little too big, you stand in my mind, dressed in smoke, reminding me of the love that I would have swallowed madness for time and time again.

> Yet there's this leak in my bathroom
> and it's dripping to the rhythm of my tears
> to the crescendo of the last time I'll let myself cry for you.

On Listening to Nick Cave's "Jubilee Street"

There's a picture of Jim Morrison hanging on my bedroom wall, and I'm naked in bed, eyes closed, while a Nick Cave record plays in my living room. The taste of nicotine and red wine sits on my tongue while I reacquaint myself with my body, two fingers deep, down Jubilee Street, and it's cold outside but I leave the window open, keep my doors unlocked.

And there's a stillness to the rhythm, to the in-and-out, to the *just a little deeper*, and I remember liking my body at one point, remember thinking it was a weapon, something that I could take out when I felt like it and use to my satisfaction. But it's different now, now that I'm alone, now that I'm sitting here wondering if I can ever scream again without seeing your face, if I can ever come again without crying and wondering where you are.

The record needs to be flipped, but Jim is looking at me telling me I can't stop—*not yet*—so I hum the melody and tell myself that I'm not in love, that I deserve love, that I am capable of love, and some of that is true, and some of it's not. I'm wet but I can't orgasm, and I turn off the music in my head and lay there, empty, bed unmade, lights turned off. It's dark here in Pittsburgh but I hold on to hope, remind myself that something beautiful always comes out of the dark, and when I wake up begging for the sound of your voice, each day hurts a little less, each second, a little more.

On the Other Side of the Glass

Outside my window, there are birds that stare at me with
snapped necks and broken wings, their beady eyes a hypnosis,
a silent control that speaks to me to let them in, to give them
a home, to mend their injuries with the soul food that I've
been feeding my heart to stay alive for the past eight months,
but they don't know I'm poisoned, don't know I killed myself
long after my trip ended that cold winter morning, and the life they see
is an illusion, a mirage to mask the death that's grayed my hair,
that's sunken my eyes, and the knife in my throat is my necklace,
a reminder that all things beautiful end in pain,
that the birds outside my window are dead, and the lot of us,
we're just stuck here waiting, punished for believing there was
something better waiting for us on the other side of the glass.

Outside While I Waited

The smell of cigarette smoke in my hair,
the jangle of change in my pocket from the
Walmart self-service line,
a stick covered in my urine
chased with too much water,
with too much beer,
the next nine months in limbo,
the number to a free clinic
scrawled on the inside of my palm
begging me to call it,
your voice in my head
telling me that this could work,
that I was special, that you loved me
but I waited outside alone,
wondering who you were sleeping with that night
as I sat there crying
to my brother on the phone,
him telling me it would be okay,
that I was strong enough to handle this myself,
just like I did with everything else

Past-Life Regression Therapy, c. 1800

She told me to close my eyes,
to think about when it started—when all the death began—
and I was a little girl running through a field of flowers,
my hair tied back with a ribbon, a blue ribbon—my favorite color in all my
    lives—
and in my hand was a compass, and in my head was a woman screaming,
telling me not to go into the woods, to stay away from the hunter,
but I was covered in leaves and dirt, my cheek cut and bleeding
and I ran, ran straight into his arms, and he put an iron cross in my hand,
told me that it twisted because that's the path we would follow,
from rebirth to death, that we'd always find our way back,
and then his knife was in my stomach,
and I was in the chair, gasping, crying, pleading,
because his eyes were the same as the man I loved
and the cross was in my bag, wrapped in his bandana,
and somehow I knew this wasn't over
because the hunter I knew
still mounted me in bed every night.

Pirate Gospel

I asked him if he was holding.
I asked him if he paid for dinner.
I asked him if he stole my Christmas presents.

    But the drugs spoke for him
    But the booze was my dinner
    But my Christmas present was a Plan-B pill

And

I wondered what his scars were from.
I wondered why he cried when he went to the basement.
I wondered when he would call his father back.

    But my new scars answered for me
    But the basement made me cry, too
    But my father wouldn't speak to me either

And

We fought about whose life was worse.
We fought about where we would sleep.
We fought about the best way to clean up blood.

    But there wasn't a competition
    But the answer was always together
    But the blood wouldn't go away.

Post-Traumatic Spiders

My doctor scribbled in her notepad,
"What do you want to talk about today?"
    I was already crying
    I ate all the cough drops on the table when she wasn't looking
    Her dog was asleep on my foot

I just left my one-night stand in the parking lot.

Frustration wore on her face like the foundation she forgot to wear
"Are the nightmares back?"
    I spun my ring around my thumb
    I thought about how you said I wore too much jewelry
    I tongued the scar on the inside of my cheek

The tarantulas are everywhere.

Her right foot tapped against the carpeted floor
"You know it's okay, right? That none of this is your fault?"
    I didn't believe her
    I felt its legs crawling up my shoulder
    I watched it watch me.

I could have stopped it. I could have said no.

Fifty minutes passed like fifty seconds
"Same time again next Wednesday?"
    I nodded my head
    I picked the spider off my cheek
    I swallowed the web it had spun around my mouth

The silk tasted like semen and blood.

Pressing Charges

Casting shadows against the asphalt
the glitter fell off in pieces as he hiked up my prom dress
fucked me against his car
police lights blaring in the background
as I screamed, called out to God

When they left
he took me to the golf course,
made me hold the citation while he tore off my locket
danger on his lips
adrenaline in my mouth;
the start of an addition
to punishment,
to getting caught

Pretty Little Things

She chopped off her hands and set them on the piano at night
sometimes they would sit there and rot,
most of the time she would bleed out and die
but sometimes they would play the song she wrote,
the melody she crafted at 2 a.m.
on the day her mother first threatened to kill herself.

She watched her fingers trace the keys,
little ivory teeth that sang the song of a closet hanging,
a little girl not but 11 years old
hiding from death in the music she wrote
to the final gasps of the last words she would speak:
    I'm sorry, Mommy.
    I didn't mean to always make you cry.

Quality Control

He leaned into my car
License and registration, young lady

I reached into the glove compartment,
found your wallet, your house keys

It had only been a few hours,
but it felt like days, like weeks.

I wondered if he could smell you on me,
if our sex was still fresh on my breath

He handed me my papers
I'm going to let you off with a warning—
  Just slow down next time, okay?

I nodded my head in understanding
gave a fake promise to take my time—
both with him
   and the body decaying in my trunk

Quarterly Letters Never Sent

I didn't drink often,
but every four months I'd open a bottle of Cabernet
chase it with a vile of his blood
write her a letter to remind myself
that while she existed,
I never did.

Quay's Brought Bon Jovi to Dublin

Summer of 2016, black tights and a cigarette behind my ear,
I walked into a pub, grabbed two pints of Smithwicks, curled into a corner
with a friend while a man played guitar on stage and a group of drunk
tourists danced and took off their shirts to his voice.

It was hot, too hot, my sweater loose but still in the way when he struck
a familiar chord, sang a favorite tune, and I was in the air, screaming,
singing with a house full of people in Temple Bar because
Bon Jovi was in the room and we were all *livin' on a prayer*, all trying
to find something halfway around the world, all trying to get by and
remove whatever broke us.

    And my voice cracked trying to reach notes on the ceiling but
    I didn't care, didn't worry about who was watching, whose hands
    were on my hips, and I smiled in my black dress, my shirt on the
    ground, my heels scuffing the floor, and when I walked back to Trinity,
    dancing on cobblestone streets, smiling at the half-moon, I laughed, laughed
    hard all the way to my room because it took me 3,427 miles to know
    what I've known all along—that it's all going to be okay.

Quit the Night, Lick the Morning

Blackened by the soot of early morning weeping,
she eased out her eyes from their sockets
placed them in her mouth
tonguing at corneas,
licking her irises

Come dawn, her vision would be clean,
a new sight for a new day,
free of nightmares,
washed fresh from torture,
she blinked emptiness away

Quoting My Dead Angels

Next to the tracks, my jacket on the ground,
I wondered what my cousin's last thought was before he chopped off his head,
what my uncle thought about before he passed away too soon,
my aunt weeping at his bedside as she held my grandmother's hand

    My angels died when I was in seventh grade
    I didn't have anyone to talk to when everyone around me started to die
    the world went quiet, and with it, so did my heart

Next to the tracks, my back against the ground
I wondered what my first love thought about on Sunday mornings,
what the man who kissed me goodbye in Ireland thinks about when he plays
    piano,
his hands gliding along the keys, the memory of my breath against his neck

    My conscience is silent, a dull static at 27
    there's a simple regret of what I do instead of what I don't
    I quote the seraphim that abandoned me and my right to pray

I'm in between the tracks now, my tailbone against metal bars
I wondered what my boyfriend thought about when I told him about the gun
what my best friend felt when I told her I didn't want to live

    My halo is splintered, a jagged horn stuck to the tip of my skull
    I can hear the whistle, the impending death brought by light
    rest in pieces, I'll see my tormentors soon.

Raven's Rock

We hiked the trails talking about death,
about how the leaves would crumble, break,
how the air would turn cold, how our parents
didn't want a mausoleum, how he wanted to
jump out of a plane, how I wanted to disappear,
we discussed how people entered Aokigahara,
tied colored ribbons around trunks and branches
so loved ones could find their bodies,
if they chose to, if they cared, if they knew,
and before us was the overlook, a sea of tress and clouds
beckoning us to jump, to swim, to breathe in the infinite
and we sat on the edges of rocks and laughed,
because now that we were there, now that it was possible,
all we wanted to do was live.

Reasons I Don't Ride Motorcycles Anymore

The last time I sat on the back of a bike, my dad was driving,
but then he wasn't because we were fighting and mom was screaming
while I cried in my bedroom, my dresser
up against the door as my father stormed out

and the phone was ringing, but my brother didn't answer it,
didn't pick it up because he was afraid, and I never heard it
because I was yelling in my closet with an old t-shirt stuffed
into my mouth

when all that time, my dad was outside bleeding, his body broken,
his head beaten in, and none of us knew that he was crawling
down a hillside begging for someone to help him,
pleading to the open field to call 911

and it was like I felt the impact of the deer when I ran outside to apologize,
when I saw the bike was missing, when I listened to the voicemail
of my dad's phone on repeat while I checked the garage, the shed,
the back porch, the garden

when all that time, the skid marks on the road were black
with his blood, blood that soaked the gurney inside the helicopter
that took him away, and I was cursing, speeding down the road,
blacked out on the way to the hospital with no memory of getting there,
my brother silent, my mother as pale as she's ever looked

and my phone was ringing, but I didn't answer it,
didn't pick it up because my dad was apologizing to me,
telling me he was sorry while they stitched up his head,
telling me he loved me while he held my hand and
promised me that he wouldn't die, that this was the last time
he'd ever ride his bike again.

Removing Past Lives

I've shed my spirit,
administered a psychological autopsy;
I'm a picture of a picture of a picture
of who I used to be.

Requiem for Love Lost and Love Gained

Whispered promises that I've heard on the tip of our tongues
slide into my ear reminding me of the plans we made
how we both said *this is it*, how the taste of each other's blood
was supposed to be the last kiss on our lips

> but I'm choking on the wine in my throat
> as I count the cigarette burns on my arms,
> each infected circle a reminder of a night
> I didn't kill myself over the loss of my future,
> now stolen away for a second time

And he's wrapping me in his arms, and it feels safe,
not like the nights you touched me when I felt cold, used,
when I wondered if there was anything sincere behind your eyes
even though I would have followed your lie to Hell

> but I'm gagging on the familiarity of it all,
> the idea of a new beginning too scary to process
> when the last one lingers against a heart littered with
> bullet holes still freshly lodged in ventricles and arteries,
> still weeping, still bleeding

Yet I'm shaking at the sound of his voice at night
as he tells me he loves me against his better judgment,
and I somehow still pray that there's feeling left in my bones,
that there's a desire to grow into the person I used to be,
into the person I know I once was, but who got lost in the scars,
who got buried in the booze and the shame

> and I'm crying in the shower over the irony of it all,
> over the fact that I couldn't protect us, and now he's protecting me,
> only I don't know how to be cared for,

how to be treated like glass when others have broken me
time and time again; a cracked ring, a shattered frame
my image no longer the face I see when I look in the mirror.

Rest Stop off of the Psycho Path

There was a knife in my dashboard
A bloody bare foot pushed the gas pedal
I sat in the passenger seat, smiling.
He drove, sweating, his chin quivering.

> You know, sometimes things don't go like we plan
> Take this moment for instance,
> I don't want to kill you
> But you're not leaving me with a whole lot of options now, are you?

There was change in my pocket
His girlfriend's purse emptied out in the back seat.
I took a sip from my silver flask.
He mumbled, prayed under his breath

> You know, it's me you should be talking to, right?
> Apologizing, making amends
> That's what makes this so easy
> You deserve this, every mile, every inch of it.

The sign said "You are now leaving Pennsylvania"
The bone in his left arm shone in the street light
I removed the knife, stabbed him in the thigh
He didn't bother to scream, just sucked in air

> You know, I think there's a rest stop up ahead,
> Pull over and get out of the car
> You're going to kill the first person you see
> I'll watch and if you do well, we'll keep driving

He shook his head, nervous-like, but he understood
I ate cheap candy corn, watched him limp toward the car

The parking lot was nearly empty,
Just a skinny loner passed out in the front seat of his Trans Am

> *You know, each kill will earn you another 100 miles,*
> *So do it quick, and make it count*
> *Oh, and just remember,*
> *All of this blood, it's on your hands, not mine.*

The radio blared a sultry Tom Waits
The steering wheel was covered with blood
He mouthed the lyrics against the wind that slapped his face
I laughed, tapped my knuckles against the window

> *You know, I find you hottest after you kill someone*
> *After you follow orders, obey*
> *You got a couple extra hours now,*
> *Let's make the best of them, shall we?*

Runaway Bride

She looked white, pale, ghastly,
and it had nothing to do with her wedding dress,
torn and wet, half-shredded and trailing behind her,
no, she looked sickly, ill, *wrong*
but I couldn't ignore her flagging me down,
her arms waving, her screams muted
by the volume of my radio as I pulled off
the side of the road.

There was dirt caked to her shoe,
only one because the other was in her hand,
heel cracked, broken like the promise she wore
on her ring finger. She was crying, screaming
as she beat on my window, her nails split,
leaving lines of blood streaking against the glass.

I eased down the window, just an inch or two,
asked her if she was okay, if I could call someone for help
but she put her mouth inside the slit, the scent of death
billowing into the passenger seat, and out dropped a stream,
a steady plop of maggots, little off-white yellowed tears
that squirmed on my floor as I sunk deeper into my seat,
scared, frozen, stiff, my foot on the gas,
my hands shaking as I tried to shift from park to drive.

Outside, the fog wrapped her in heavy arms, her eyes black,
her teeth sharp, pointed like individual stakes, but I swallowed panic,
shifted to survival, drove away from the girl,
from the woman in the white dress, leaving her stranded and able,
hungry for a ride, for a body, for someone to help her,
and maybe they would, but maybe they wouldn't,
either way, the maggots and I didn't care

because we both managed to escape.

Second Place to a Musician's First Love

His guitar case was crammed under my bed
while a drug test marinated on my bathroom sink,
my piss coming up negative, my future looking positive,
my parents screaming, my phone buzzing,
him calling to have me meet him at the party,
to wear something light, something that he could
easily slip his hands under, something that I wouldn't mind
getting wet, getting soaked, getting licked off me
under the stars and I was running and driving
singing to the tune of his lips against mine,
and when he took out his guitar, he smiled,
said that's my girl, not talking to me.

Seduced by Monsters

There's a crocodile in my bed
a merman in my shower
and sometimes when I leave my apartment
I feel your hand on my shoulder,
your breath on my neck,
a story I've read a thousand times,
one that I can't seem to shake,
can't seem to put to sleep
because there's a madman in my closet,
a sociopath between my legs
and there's no remedy for the bite on my shoulder,
to the vampire that drains me at night,
to the wolfman who eats my heart
because I share my home with nightmares
open my door to fiends,
and I have no one to blame but myself
when the lights out go,
when I start to scream,
when I realize that sometimes,
yes, sometimes,
monsters are just monsters,
and nothing more.

Self-Study in Pornography

I've been doing a self-study in porn to try and learn about sex. I've acted, I've directed, I've sat in a corner and watched, and it's funny to me how people who don't even know each other find ways to connect, when the people I've loved for years can't fuck me because they find it painful. My vagina is tired from the excuses, my clit, sandpaper from an absent touch, and I can't get off anymore: no matter what I watch, no matter who is inside me, no matter what I fantasize about. The end result is always the same. I'm

Dry
    Dry
        Dry

So I tried masturbating on the side of the road on my way home from work. I tried locking myself in the bathroom and pretending I still live at my parent's. At night, I'd sit outside on the porch, one hand down my pants, the other holding my cigarette, and I'd smoke and cry while my boyfriend talked on the phone to the woman he was cheating on me with. It used to bother me that I couldn't orgasm, that my sex turned me into this, but I can't *feel* like I used to anymore. Not with my body. Not with my heart. Inside I'm

Dead
    Dead
        Dead

And as I lay sprawled out on this stranger's bed, his camera clicking away while he rubs between his legs, while his spits onto my slit, I wonder if my lovers— the ones I actually loved—ever think about the contagions they planted in my head each time they told me I wasn't good enough, that they couldn't look at me, that touching me made them sick, because I think of what it's like to fuck me now, how I get frustrated, how I bleed. I can't love without love, but my heart no longer pumps, and the more I sleep around, the worse the nightmares get. I'm drowning in black and white Polaroids, I'm immortalized in 30 second video clips, and each time I make eye contact with the camera, I think of you, and I think of me, and I

    Cry
        Cry
            Cry

Sheet Music to My Acoustic Nightmare

We were in turmoil, obsessed, possessed, there was beer and there were darts, and I spent hours in the bathroom stall crying next to where someone had carved your name into the wood. I started smoking then, then next to the statue of the giant toad behind the bar, the bar where we first met, where you told me you were Romanian, where you put your ring on my finger—the ring I still wear—where you asked me if I wanted to be a pirate, if I wanted to be a gypsy,

and I remember thinking that this me was the real me, not the version who used to bow and break and bend and say *yes*, but that this experience, this freedom to be high and excited, to be loose and reckless, to let a man take off my stockings and cover me in wine, to let an angel kiss my eyelids, to have a person walk with me in the darkness, play music to my acoustic nightmare,

and yes, there were bruises and blood, broken bones and shattered glass—I hated everything that we were, everything that we did to each other, but even still, the nights spent waking up in trees and standing on rooftops in winter, the breaking into marble factories dressed like Janis Joplin, the dreadlocks you let me put into your hair, those are the moments I remember now, the softness, the gentleness, the times when you lit candles in the room, when you told me sex wasn't something you needed to fall in love, when you fell to the ground and begged me to stay, when I picked you up on the side of the road, guitar in hand, panic in your pocket—

those moments remind me that you held me while I cried, that you forgave me when I ran away, that when I tried to hide and disappear, that you came after me that New Year's night, that you fought for me during graduation, trusted me with your fears for our future, and now I'll never hear your voice again, never laugh with you in the flowers or drive into the mountains to listen to your stories under blankets of cigarette smoke and dead leaves, so

I cry a lot to the memory of your face, and maybe we both need this pain—to be each other's biggest regret—because I know that those months spent with you made me strong, made me soft, made me believe in love and hate, in angels and demons, and I'm sorry, and I forgive you, but I broke, and I came back, and wanted dead or alive, my bonfire heart still sings your sheet music every day in this nightmare we built trying to chase the horizon in each other's arms, because all of this is for you: every word, every song, every pillage, every curse. You'll forever be the dead man walking inside my head.

She Filled a Music Box Full of Bad Dreams

The songs of yesterday played on repeat in her head—
a mess of gothic hymns about lost lockets
and a promise ring she drowned in the woods
when she ran away five winters ago.
And there's a music box on her dresser that rewinds itself each night;
a present reminder that certain melodies can't be unsung
no matter how many time she attempts to murder their lyrics

but still she reaches for the locket and finds a noose instead—
a carefully knotted circle frayed at the edges
resembling the split ends of the hair she stopped cutting
when he faded away five springs ago.
And there's a music box on her dresser that whispers prayers to her each night;
a present reminder that some words are better left unspoken
no matter how many ribs she breaks when she cries into the dark

yet she can't shut off the tune that beats inside her blood—
a poisonous cocktail of self-doubt and name calling
that she can't force herself to unhear
when she locks herself in the bathroom each May.
And there's a music box on her dresser that laughs at her each night;
a present reminder of the wedding song she'd never dance to
with the man who wasn't strong enough to stay by her side.

The Fireworks Were Wet in 2011

It was the Fourth of July and I was sitting at home, alone, working on my manuscript. I hadn't eaten that day, but Jack Daniels filled me full. My boyfriend was drunk in a park, not answering my calls. My best friend posted a picture of him and her on Facebook. I continued to write about devils, continued to get drunk. I called again. No answer. I took off my clothes. Wrote naked. Drank pain. I looked at the picture of them some more, etched it in my memory. I woke up in my bathtub hours later. My skin looked blue. I was freezing and my hair was clumped together in thick strands of black tangled knots. My phone, on the countertop, rang and rang and rang. I answered it—my throat burning—and he said that he was sick of me playing victim. That if I wanted to die, I should just do it. I hung up, checked my messages. "I hope she's worth it. Don't let my brother find me." At least I didn't say "I love you" before I tried to drown myself to sleep. Dignity. I still had my pride. I dried off, walked back to my desk, kept writing about devils, but that time, I wrote about me.

The First Time I Thought of Suicide, I was on the Toilet

One day in eighth grade
my best friend tripped me in the lunch line;
everyone pointed and laughed at my skinned knee,
at my flushed cheeks painted with embarrassment,
stained with ketchup.

I picked up my tray of food I couldn't eat,
let the spilled juice mix with the humiliation
I left on the floor;

I went and sat in the bathroom stall alone,
crying as I cleaned up my blood
like my mother never would.

The girls followed me,
stood at the sink. They called me a lesbian
they told me I was worthless,
asked me why I didn't go home and kill myself.

And I couldn't answer them.

There's a Gypsy in My Chest

There's a gypsy in my chest and she's screaming to be let out so I walk the fire, embrace the stars, I draw the lover card and I am Death, Death, named by the hands of fate, surrounded by swords, by cups, I wear a pentacle around my neck for good fortune but still she screams because the card that reminds me of the boy is tucked inside my bra close to my heart so I remember that he's why my soul is bleeding, the reason that I have to caravan my way back to the desert, back to the woods, back to where my life started, to where the jazz was smooth but rough enough to make me dance, to where I was hypnotized by the flutes, by the drums, made to sing songs that had yet to be written, to drink wine that begged to be drunk, and now I sleep under a blanket of constellations and planets, whispering prayers to whoever will listen, and I wander and wander trying out different lives, different people, thinking maybe I'd forget him, and maybe I wouldn't, but maybe fate had something different in store for me, something else that Death could only one day hope to devour.

The Moon Makes Love to Shadows

I pin my shadow to the moon and there's my silhouette
Covered in darkness and dust;
I spit the cool blackness out of my mouth
And inside my lungs grow teeth.
They swallow and purge the graveyard air inside
And laugh a wheeze that smells like dead violets.
I dance there under my mistress,
Naked and smooth as the day I was born,
My body glistening under the light of the stars
Reverberating like an echo, like a vibrating slab of flesh.
I want to kiss her
Make love to the earth below
But I am nothing but an image of the person I used to be,
I am static, a whisper
And the new moon is the only one who knows my body.

Two of Swords

It's still suffocating
These memories,
These images in my head—
I cut the deck,
Swallow my pride.
My cards are sharp
With crying towers
And lovers who have never seen hearts.
There's smoke coming from the eyes
Of the woman holding two blades crisscrossed against her chest,
Her neck slit in invisible haste as conflict broods
In her taut, stitched lips.
I sigh.
My throat swells from words I cannot speak.

Why does the moon hate the way I breathe?
The universe despise the way I love?

I touch the cards, a Vitruvian spread
That spits fire at my future,
Weaving madness,
Spilling blood,
And my stars align in Hell,
While Aries, my ram,
Runs into the same wall
Over and over and over again;
A stubborn beast who
Makes the same mistakes,
Cries the same tears,
Kills the same dreams,
And I sit there and watch,
A bystander to what fate has foretold,

A destiny written in storms,
Forged in spilled ink and lost treasures,
And I am the mistress to all things forgotten
Things that were
And things that never shall be.

Ugly Little Things, Aren't They?

The mirror watched me as I cried,
my reflection a second-me, the real me,
the version of myself I felt most at peace with,
that I embraced naked, vulnerable, the less-than-pleasant image
that made him sleep alone, that made him turn away, and oh,
these tears—*ugly little things, aren't they?*—how they dripped,
how they fell down my cheeks in black balloons,
like individual deflated dreams butchered at your hand
with the looking glass you broke to teach me a lesson,
to remind me that some things hurt worse than words,
but the black and blue imprint on my chest tells me that you're wrong,
that words are like cigarette burns in my brain, a black fire,
like acid in my eyes, each blink a breath of sorrow and ash,
a proclamation of pain, a devotion to the eggshells I walk on,
especially when you tell me to smile.

Under Take Her

He painted my cheeks with rouge,
dabbed a nude shade of pink on my lips
I didn't like the way I looked,
so fake, doll-like, a mere reflection of my former self
but he took me to his room,
sat me in his reading chair, propped up,
my glasses on, my hair freshly curled,
formaldehyde running through my veins

I don't remember how I got here,
I just remember rain and sleet and the hum of my car
but now he's underneath me, inside me, next to me
a taking of body, of flesh
my voice silenced, my fists unclenched,
there's no fighting back once you're dead.

Under the Dirt Blanket

When I died, I wanted to be cremated
but here I am, awake in this coffin,
an eternity of darkness
with the silent movies in my head,
and the boys think that I'm lights out,
that I can't hear them digging me up,
can't feel them pulling me out of my box—

But those bastards
still fuck me in my grave,
just like they raped me into my death,
and the light of the moon is blinding,
the sound of their grunts and groans much too loud,
my limbs lifeless, my heart, no longer beating
so the pain of their sex doesn't hurt me like it did
when they took my virginity away,
when they ate my innocence in the woods,

Yet this time, I'm angry,
my body a rebellion of wasps and worms
I spit maggots in their mouths,
stain their cocks with bloodied dirt
and death appeases me
because I never have to come for them again,
because I never have to be betrayed by the body
that moistened when all I wanted was to cry,

They shove me back in my wooden prison,
a sex doll two-weeks dead;
I watch the movie on repeat behind my eyes
knowing that in a few years, I'll be gone,
nothing left but bones and dust,

and they won't have anything
to take from me anymore.

Unwelcomed Decisions on the 5:30 p.m. Blue Line

He limped up and down the train
his left leg cut, bleeding into his untied shoe
I moved my gym bag
He sat down, slept against the metal headrest
of the seat in front of him
while blurred faces and fluorescent lights
passed by us on the other side
of the frosted glass;
such deformed expressions
laughing manically
at the man too weak to stand,
at the girl too trusting
of the knife wound to his thigh.

Unwinding the Black Outs

Unwinding the black outs,
I found a stream of karaoke nights,
laughs around the jukebox,
Adderall highs and smoke rings,
champagne bottles and poker chips,
but flashback after flashback brought the pain,
the incendiary stab to the place in my memory
where I kept you hidden,
where I allowed you to live,
yet in my nightmares, you're escaping,
bringing back reels of film, playing movies on repeat
forcing me to watch, to partake in scenes
where we slept in tunnels curled up near boilers,
where we ate ice cream while watching *Labyrinth*,
me imitating the puppets,
you mixing cocktails in the back
telling me to stop talking,
to listen to the movie
but I found the lyrics
to the song you wrote me,
a ring from one of your plays,
the bracelet you stole for me
while we thrift shopped
in your hometown
the day that I called in sick
because my tires were slashed,
because I was high and drunk,
strung out in the woods,
puking in the movie theatre
while Maleficent laughed,
talked about cursed little girls
and you held my hand,

told me to suck it up,
that I looked paler than usual.

Validated PTSD, Therapy Session #4

I gave him the key to my apartment,
triggered myself to the memory of a message in a bottle,
of the code to my lockbox hidden in a poem that sat on the table
in your kitchen next to the picture of us that I had framed

And

I choked on the word 'love,'
triggered myself back to the time
I thought I would get married,
where I walked the streets of Dublin
giving tours of Trinity College,
watching the sunrise with him on my iPad,
looking at engagement rings
with a man who would break my heart

And

I thought about the shower,
how I used to cry against the tiles,
my mascara streaked down my face while I
I tried to masturbate in the water, tried to trick myself
into being wet, into feeling something other than the loss of self
I felt every time I looked in the mirror
and stared at the body you'd turned me to hate

And

What was I thinking, here, in in this parking lot,
on this gravel road that kissed my kneecaps
as I sobbed praying near the stop sign,
triggering to the moment I imagined myself

flying off the edge of the Cincinnati Bridge,
my lungs filling with water,
just like my aunt's on the night of her suicide.

And

What was I doing, here, in this shower
licking the blood of my freshly slit wrists
as I screamed to the image of your eyes
looking back at me in the dim of the candlelight
that illuminated my bathroom purple like the
color of the flowers I put in our memory box

Valkyrie Training for the Day

Accompanied by ravens,
I watched the battlefield
erupt in clouds of red and pink,
a flutter of skin, a feathering of bone,
voices cracking, screams fading
pleas for death, for life, for love
echoing all around while

the black birds spoke to me,
told me stories about deception,
about fights born out of jealousy,
a lying tongue, a butchered heart,
cries of pain, of ecstasy, of torment
stuck like fishing hooks
inside their mouths because

I was still deciding,
a careful choosing of survival
a passing moment to end abuse,
to solidify intent, to modify motive
through my criteria of punishment
through elimination of breath.

Verifying Bodies After Car Crashes

On the side of the road,
I waited for split metal, for burnt rubber,
the sound of screaming, of bones cracking,
steam on my face, blood on my jeans
the area between my legs wet with excitement,
moist with fear.

The September air hung loose,
a crisp death soon filled the exhaust,
soon clung to the mirrors, to the windows,
while I rubbed my body
against mangled pieces of flesh and steel.

I took their licenses,
hid them in my back pocket
before the police came, before the ambulance showed up,
played friend, played family so it seemed like I belonged,
like I wasn't waiting around for death,
like I wasn't getting off on gravel tattoos,
on asphalt scars, on seatbelt sutures.

But before the lights and the sirens,
I gushed orgasm over tangled limbs,
over crushed lungs and ruptured spleens,
the adrenaline still hot on my tongue
when they questioned me,
the thrill still pumping my blood
when I verified their bodies.

Versions of My Mutilated Self

My self-portrait is off,
off like the version who smokes in abandoned houses
off like the version who slips into the black
off like the version who whispers into palms
      pulls magic from the stars
      takes curses from the earth
      licks afterlife from the graves

My self-portrait is bleeding,
bleeding like the artery I accidentally hit
bleeding like the words I used to try to get you to stay
bleeding like the girl who lives in her memories
      hears voices long past gone
      feels pain inside her walls
      sleeps with monsters in her dreams

My self-portrait is bone,
bone like the calcium I have to take to get better
bone like the leg I shattered on the road
bone like the color of my hospital walls
      Yelling for you to let me out
      Begging for you to come back
      Pleading for you to stay away

Because this self-portrait is better,
Better like the bleached floorboards of my home
Better like the missing organs in their chests
Better like the dying flowers on my desk

screaming about absence
crying about pain
laughing about emptiness

the emptiness of it all.

Violins Bring the Serpents

He stood playing violin in the middle of the road.
I danced in my red dress, the one that blossomed like a flower
when I spun in circles, pretending to be innocent.

I'd watch him work the strings as the music filled my head.
My brown curls weaving themselves between my fingers
as I let the rhythm of the song climb inside me.

And there were snakes at my feet, serpents around my neck.
My body shook itself possessed, the sound of hissing,
the sound of tradition pulling me deeper in with the spirits

    somewhere down in Congo Square.

Wearing Red Lipstick and Skyping with the Wolf

Like the first time I had sex,
I didn't know how to Skype until he showed me.

I thought you talked face-to-face
not groin-to-groin

but there was my clit,
pink, swollen, and on camera;
a rediscovered loss of virginity.

He told me when to take off my clothes,
how to drop them like tears to the floor, and

I'd spend 15 minutes getting ready before I'd call
so my lipstick looked extra red on camera

so when the light hit my face
you couldn't see my fear.

What I Brought with Me on the Plane

An iron cross.
The necklace he made for me on our second date.
A rusted skull ring.
A black bandana.
The rosary I bought in Rome.
A worry stone made of rose quartz.
A toothbrush.
My anxiety.
A bottle of pills.
Notebook and pen.

What it Takes to Sing the Blues

There's a canary in my ribcage
and she's dying, rattling against
my ivory bars with her death songs
and her high-pitched wails. I want to
reach inside and strangle her—finish
the job for the winged beast
I swallowed for my career,
but there's something about the
tone of her death that gives my voice a rasp,
a touch of melancholy that brings audiences to tears, and all it takes
is my lying down on the piano while she suffocates, wheezes, and hacks,
and then, and only then, can I properly sing the blues.

When I Promised Him Murder

For Wayne

Whiskey stained my notebook, he stained my lips
I pushed my hair behind my ear, thought about pulling it up,
    about letting the ravens out
but I sat there, legs crossed, stockings ripped
my curls settling on my shoulders
while I played with the ring I won in a bet
two years ago from a bar down the street.

And

The lights were down
The people were watching
    and yet I couldn't stop remembering
    couldn't stop seeing how this would play out:
    him pressed against me: my hand on his cheek.

But

Music filled the bar, his tongue, my mouth
I wrote poetry to the sound of his vocal chords,
    lyrics to the melodies he'd strum on my body
and when he walked away, hair down, body tense
I'd smile with the vibrations that danced in the room
my words searing, my phrases piercing, him unknowing
as they slid down his throat like a reverse-siren song

And

The lights were down
The people were watching
    and yet I couldn't stop remembering

  couldn't stop seeing how this would play out
    breathless and panting: my hand on his cheek

And

Death stained my fingertips, his blood, my hands
I smoothed out my dress, reapplied my lipstick
  careful to get the perfect shade of red,
the bar was closing, but I was already gone,
my venom toxic, a well-hidden drug.

And

The lights were down
The people were watching
  and yet I couldn't stop remembering
  couldn't stop seeing how this would play out
  stiff and sorry: my hand on his cheek

Winter Canvas

Winter is a dust-covered palette,
a cumulus memory
in diluted ink;
it survives in blacks and grays,
in crows and fresh ash,
and I paint a forest of trees as barren as I am,
their branches like arthritic arms
holding me against the wind
but it hurts and
I cough on icicles,
see my breath on its canvas,
an impasto of sickness and age;
I use its solstice brush to smear
charcoal against the sky,
a chiaroscuro background of
feathers and soot
yet while blended and blurred,
a path evolves towards spring
and I curve it out of darkness,
make it bone,
virginal in asylum-white,
but this blank madness is a snow bank,
a chest of clouds that hold the secret to rebirth
to second chances,
but it's too bright for my sorrow
so I cover it, too, in shadows
of storm,
in a thunderous moor
uncontained by page
by season
or by art,
and now I can sleep,
sleep sound and sleep tight,

hibernate with snowflakes
that kiss my hair like serpents,
curl up with the wind that
screams my dreams
into nightmares.

Yawning While Driving Down '61

I dipped myself in the concrete sludge of sleep,
a haze of 2 a.m. hallucinations down the highway
while a dead girl flagged me down on the side of the road,
told me to stop and take a nap with her,

but I drove on, yawning, inhaling the asphalt spirits,
my music too loud, the wind too cold,
home hundreds of miles away with nothing but a dead-end job,
a pile of dirty laundry, a sink full of crusted dishes
waiting for me to return

I saw her again two hours later, still in the same blue dress,
still with the same bloodied mouth, her right arm broken,
a pick-axe in the small of her back,
but this time, I pulled over,
opened my door and invited her in

and suddenly the world didn't seem so dark,
not now that I had someone to share the nightmare with.

Yearly Bath for a Tired Heart

Once a year, every year,
I take out my heart, put it in a porcelain bowl in the sink,
wash it with chamomile and lavender,
let it soak in a bath of warmth
so for just a few minutes a year,
it knows what it feels like to relax,
to be held and loved,
to not be in so much pain.

Yelling in My Sleep

I'm sweating through my blankets,
and there's nightmare on my tongue
an incubus on my stomach
a horse gnawing on the split ends of my hair
as his head pokes through the frosted glass
of my dripping window while tree branches
pound like hammers against the siding of my house

There's a sound in the corner of my bedroom
a slow clap, the slapping of wet lips
I recognize the scent of burning myrrh
the smell of mistletoe and blood
because she's watched me since I was a little,
always present yet hidden, a steady mirage
her breath tickling my neck even though
she's never touched me, not once, not yet

But now my t-shirt is soaked
and there's drool on my pillow
dried blood caked to the inside of my nose
and I'm clawing at my wallpaper,
ripping it off in shreds, in streams,
because no one listens to me when I tell them they're here,
the insufferable demons of my dreams,
the night monsters, the rapists,
the woman who follows me hoping to
steal my soul.

Young Wolves Take to the Night

A hungry abandonment in this scarred disappointment,
I put the bandages over my eyes, follow her down to the water

She drinks from the river, an insatiable thirst
I break glass against my body to see if I still bleed

There's a full moon out as we scavenge the earth
two souls of the same ancestry, we walk the night;
a growl lodged in the throat song of our people

Blind to darkness, deaf to screams
the two of us bound by family, by curse

as we shift into our other selves
taking turns between animal and man,
hunter and hunted; we break time and time again

Your Ghost

You live in my bookshelves,
in the spaces between the walls where my nails raked the plaster,
where my screams went to hide when it all got to be too much;

there are parts of you under my doormat,
stuffed between the cushions of the couch that I burned,
lodged somewhere deep inside my purple backpack,
the one I threw in the river after our last night.

Yes, you live in my mouth,
in the taste of honey and freshly ground mint
on the edge of burnt toast and coffee grinds
from the roasted beans I threw out six months ago;

in fact, there are pieces of you still stuck in my throat,
wedged in the lining of my stomach,
swimming in my self-induced vomit
from when I tried to purge the memory of your tongue.

Yet inside me, you multiply, flourish,
like infected seedlings pumping poison through my veins
the essence of you bubbling in my blood,
forever reminding me that you're here to stay,
that you're not leaving any time soon.

Zero Regrets Party Crashing

I wasn't supposed to be there
but I snuck in through the back,
and no one noticed me
as I put in a request at the piano,
ordered a double shot of whiskey, neat
from the bartender whose accent was so thick
I could hardly understand him

I nodded and sipped my drink,
Jim Morrison's lyrics filling the bar
when a man came up to me,
put a drink with a wet fig in front of me
told me to show him what it looked like
to finger me here on this velvet couch

My friends laughed, I spit out my drink,
and then everyone was fingering figs on the table
laughing about feminism, about scissoring
because it was our last night together
and come tomorrow morning,
none of us could pretend that we weren't
who we really were anymore.

Zest for the Afterbite

In leather boots and fishnet stockings,
I slipped out of my jean jacket,
the music blaring, the bass dropping,
my friends tripping on Molly as they danced
against the backdrop of the black and white films
that played on the concrete wall.

My neck was sore from the biting,
but my lips tasted like rust and strawberries
like copper and blackberry jam,
and he was like midnight, like velvet
in the way his hand rested on my waist,
the subtle nuances of both a gentleman
and a vicious lover.

I didn't know I was dead until the next day,
34 missed calls, my eyes two sunken holes
against the pale pallor of my skin,
but he smiled as he dressed my wounds,
traced the scratch marks down my back
told me I wouldn't need the drugs anymore,
that feeding the hunger was the best high to chase

Zigzagging Through Asylum Snowflakes

Outside the window, the world was blanketed white, and he was telling me about the time his grandmother worked in an asylum, and I was telling him about the last time I was in love, and I drank and giggled, tried to smile, but the drinks were catching up with me, and the tattoos on his body were moving, fluttering, and as we walked back to our cars, I realized that the love story I told him was about the first time I heard him read one of his poems—the one about the house being abandoned, lost, the metaphor of a broken relationship—but he didn't hear me when I told him I thought he was beautiful, and I didn't think my heart could ache like that again, but I was wrong, and I was cold, and the snowflakes in my hair made me think about the time that I locked myself in the asylum: it was the first time I, too, stopped hearing anything about love.

Ziploc Bag Full of Dead Butterflies

In the second drawer from the bottom,
that's where I keep them:
my pinned and desiccated beauties,
my treasure trove of insect bodies
dried and withering away into multi-colored dust.

See, I've stitched their wings together
sewed them by color, by pattern,
an exquisite collection of corpses for study
a plastic morgue filled with the deaths
of God's most delicate creatures.

At night, I sometimes hear them rustling,
trying to work together to fly away, to resurrect
but the glue that holds their carcasses together,
the adhesive that binds them one by one,
that weighs them down in suffocating bliss,
will keep them preserved for me for quite some time,
that is, until I go through my own metamorphosis,
through my own rebirth of night sky and blood.

Zombie-Syndrome in a Foreign City

Moving through crowds, dead on my feet
I shuffled through street acts and protestors,
through walking advertisements, homeless men
who harassed me in the streets, grabbing for my purse

I walked on

A watery glaze covering my eyes, bloodshot, blurry
the world around me in constant movement
while I floated down the highway of my mind
While vendors stuck flyers in my hands, coupons in my pocket

I never noticed

The inability that people have with speaking to one another
my cell phone buzzing, immediately turned silent
I hung up on the skype call from my boyfriend
yawned as I got on the train, put my head against the window

I instantly slept

The constant buzz of tracks vibrating my thoughts
locked and loaded in this city I've never been to
and I had no idea where I was or where I was going
but I wondered if it really mattered as the hallucinogenic lights
glowed in the reflection of the window, luring me deeper into my lost

About the Author

STEPHANIE M. WYTOVICH IS AN American poet, novelist, and essayist. Her work has been showcased in numerous anthologies such as *Gutted: Beautiful Horror Stories*, *Shadows Over Main Street: An Anthology of Small-Town Lovecraftian Terror*, *Year's Best Hardcore Horror: Volume 2*, *The Best Horror of the Year: Volume 8*, as well as many others.

Wytovich is the Poetry Editor for Raw Dog Screaming Press, an adjunct at Western Connecticut State University and Point Park University, and a mentor with Crystal Lake Publishing. She is a member of the Science Fiction Poetry Association, an active member of the Horror Writers Association, and a graduate of Seton Hill University's MFA program for Writing Popular Fiction. Her Bram Stoker Award-winning poetry collection, *Brothel*, earned a home with Raw Dog Screaming Press alongside *Hysteria: A Collection of Madness*, *Mourning Jewelry*, and *An Exorcism of Angels*. Her debut novel, *The Eighth*, is published with Dark Regions Press.

Follow Wytovich at http://www.stephaniewytovich.com/ and on twitter @Swytovich.